By Their Fruits

The Lasting Impact of Toronto in the UK

WORD PUBLISHING

WORD ENTERTAINMENT LTD
Milton Keynes, England

BY THEIR FRUITS

ISBN 1-86024-396-7

Unless otherwise indicated, biblical quotations are from
the New King James Version, © 1982 by Thomas Nelson, Inc.

Produced for Word Publishing by
Bookprint Creative Services, PO Box 827, BN21 3YJ, England.
Printed in Great Britain.

BY THEIR FRUITS

CONTENTS

FOREWORD

I remember being very surprised at the number of leaders and laymen from Britain that began visiting Toronto in 1994. We hosted meetings where the majority of those present were from somewhere in the UK. It was a reflection of the deep hunger for more of the Lord that was growing in Great Britain. The word was out – God was moving in Toronto. Because it was in Canada, and not the US, it was, perhaps, a little easier for some Brits to come over and see for themselves. We are indebted to these hungry folks, who returned home raving about the 'blessing' that they had received in Toronto. The British press soon labelled what was happening, the 'Toronto Blessing'. Friends told friends, and more came: the hungry, the desperate, the discouraged and the sceptical, and God met them in a powerful way. They came searching for greater anointing, more power, or greater success in ministry yet, instead, received closeness and intimacy with a loving heavenly father. It became obvious that we need to fulfil the 'great commandment' (Matt. 22:37) before we will fulfil the 'great commission' (Matt. 28:19). Hundreds of leaders and then churches were thereby greatly impacted by the overwhelming love of God.

Over the years, this love has nurtured a hunger for revival, which has not abated, in the UK. Many are still hungering and thirsting for a national awakening, which we have not yet seen.

But I believe that the seeds for such an awakening are in the soil and are growing: the ongoing ripple effect will be phenomenal, with millions coming to Christ.

In my opinion, the lasting impact of 'Toronto' has yet to be determined, yet already the personal lives and ministries of many leaders has been deeply affected by this wonderful infilling of the Holy Spirit. How do you put a value on a life transformed forever by the power of God? The heart of an individual gains so much through experiencing the Father's love, acceptance and forgiveness. Deep emotional healing has taken place, as well as an impartation of gifting and envisioning. Leaders have emerged from their Toronto experience embracing a more healthy and passionate pursuit of the Kingdom of God. Most can testify that they are not at all in the same place as they were in 1994 and 1995. The changes and growth in ministry and effectiveness are remarkable. The church today is not the same place as it was seven years ago. People now come expecting God to be in the meeting in a real and powerful way. All of us in Toronto are extremely thankful to God to have been able to play a small part in seeing Great Britain moving closer to national revival, as many hundreds of leaders, having been deeply affected by the power of the Holy Spirit, will never be the same again.

You are about to read the personal testimonies of several well-known British leaders, whose lives will never be the same again, because of the touch of the Holy Spirit's power. May the Lord kindle a hunger and a fire in you as you seek to be filled by Him.

John Arnott, Senior Pastor
Toronto Airport Christian Fellowship

GERALD COATES

Gerald leads the Pioneer network of churches and the *Waverley Abbey House Team. He is a well-known speaker, author of nine books and a regular broadcaster on both TV and radio. Gerald is married to Anona and has three sons, Paul, Simon, and Jonathan.*

GERALD COATES

Chapter One

It was a beautiful, warm, sunny Sunday morning in May, 1994. I was driving into South West London, from my home in Esher, Surrey, to speak at the Vineyard Church led by John Mumford. I had a warm respect for John, we only live twenty minutes away from each other, but we were not close friends. So his invitation was kind and generous, and I was looking forward to the meeting. The melodies of Mozart drifted out of my car as I drew into the car park of the school building.

The greeting was friendly, the worship genuine, and introduction so flattering; I could hardly wait to meet myself! After speaking for about forty minutes, I called for people to respond and thirty or forty came forward for prayer. Some were crying, a few kneeling and one or two were lying on the floor. It even looked as though one or two were trembling. I thought to myself 'This is nothing unusual – after all this is the Vineyard!' All in all, it was a highly enjoyable morning: some unfinished business was dealt with and lives were touched and blessed.

John then took me off to lunch, somewhat mysteriously, without his wife. We took time over the menu, ordered our meal, and chatted about the weather, news items and the restaurant. 'So what's happened to you?' he asked in a somewhat pointed fashion. I was somewhat taken aback. 'What do you mean?' I replied. 'Well, we've never seen such power in a Sunday morning meeting.' I was somewhat stunned. It was a good meeting, I confess, but nothing special, other than for the few I prophesied over. I was flattered and intrigued, but the conversation nevertheless moved on. The absence of John's wife, Ellie, was a little unsettling, as was his failure to mention her. 'So how is your wife Ellie?' I hesitantly enquired. 'Oh, she's in Toronto', he replied, realising that he had forgotten to tell me. 'Oh' I responded, somewhat relieved. 'Family? Holiday?' John paused, frowned and responded: 'Haven't you heard?' He went on to explain about the Holy Spirit, falling in a very ordinary Vineyard Church. He spoke of meetings several nights a week, of hundreds and now thousands attending, and manifestations of the Holy Spirit or reactions to His presence which included shaking, laughing, falling and most importantly, confession and repentance.

I had been looking, along with various friends and colleagues, for signs of revival. Was this one of those signs? I couldn't wait to finish the meal. When it was over I jumped into my car and grabbed my cell phone to connect with Martin Scott, a leader of Pioneer People, the church I am a part of, twenty miles south west of London. I explained what I had heard. 'Martin, I believe it will happen tonight.'

I drove back down the A3 to Leatherhead on the M25, the motorway that circles London. I had explained the story as best I could, including the name of the pastor, John Arnott, the city of Toronto, and someone else who was involved by the name of Rodney Howard-Browne. But I'd added, 'I don't want these names mentioned tonight, so that if something happens we cannot be accused of the power of auto-suggestion'.

Martin gave a straightforward Christ-centred message. Then he gave an appeal for prayer, and a number of people responded. He stood on the floor of the sports hall at the left-hand side of the stage and I stood on the right. He then prayed with a businesswoman, who fell on the floor screaming with laughter! Nothing like this had ever happened before as far as I can recall. It had begun!

Little did I know the joys, growth, profile and platforms we would be given as a result of this: both in the UK and across the world. And little did I know the pain, disappointments, frustrations and failures that would accompany such blessing.

As I have already mentioned, the year was 1994. I was forty-nine years old. I had been married to Anona for twenty-seven years. We had three sons, Paul, Simon and Jonathan. I led Pioneer People, a church of several hundred people. As part of a team, I also led a network of churches and training programmes, and was becoming an adviser/pastor to singer-songwriters Noel Richards and Martin Smith of Delirious, as well as to others in the world of politics, entertainment and church leadership. We had received significant prophecies regarding revival, my involvement with the media and television, politicians, reconciliation between black and white, and discipling some of the 'movers and shakers' of society.

Life was very fulfilling, but I knew that the nation was losing the Gospel. As it happened, I was in the process of making a film about prayer and revival. John Arnott was in Brighton at a conference with several other speakers I wanted to interview. John was kind, generous, and helpful and featured in my film.

Shortly afterwards, fifty or more key leaders from the Pioneer network met and I explained what was happening in Toronto. 'Well, we can't all go there,' one of them commented, 'let's pray here'. Well we did, and chaos ensued. Piles of bodies – those with national travelling ministries, theologians, a doctor, children's workers and worship leaders – littered the floor. Others were so 'drunk' on the Spirit that they could not stand or even be held up. Noel Richards was transfixed, as in a trance. One Bible teacher looked at all this in silence, with his hands in his pockets, until what seemed to be an invisible hand knocked him sideways and he fell to the floor, without anybody touching him.

Within days, the Apostolic Team Leaders' Forum, drawing a dozen or more streams of churches together, met in the same place, not far from where our church meets. News of Toronto was everywhere. When we prayed with each other, similar scenes of laughter, tears, and apparent drunkenness filled the room. One man was prayed for and shouted out, 'Oh, no, not a shaking arm!' He then fell to the floor. Later he confessed he had been to a meeting and had been distracted by a woman sitting in front of him, whose arm had been shaking throughout the entire proceedings. He told the Lord, 'I want to be open to all of this, but I never want a shaking arm. Never again.'

The 'Toronto Blessing' had already hit the headlines of our national newspapers. Ellie had returned from Toronto, and had gathered a few pastors and leaders in her home to explain what had gone on. One of those present was a leader at Holy Trinity, Brompton, the evangelical, charismatic Anglican church in Knightsbridge, South West London. He had returned to their offices to explain where he had been. As he spoke, staff slipped off their chairs onto the floor. News of what happened travelled quickly. On Sunday, an explanation was given for what was happening, and an opportunity for prayer was given at the close of the service. The same chaos ensued. Because a number of Lords, Members of Parliament and prominent business people attend the church, and because it was considered the safe Church of England, news spread like wildfire. Press took photographs of long lines of people getting to the church building an hour or more before the service began. Conservative evangelicals reacted, 'where is this in the scriptures?' Suddenly, the very people who had promoted the revivalist Whitefield, with all of his theatrics, weeping, stomping, shaking and laughing, were in trouble. Revival is safe at a distance, 200 years ago or three thousand miles away, but what was happening here?

Eventually, I travelled to Toronto at the invitation of John Arnott, to take a part in one of their large conferences. I went with my eldest son, Paul, now aged thirty-one. Thousands gathered to worship, with a high level of expectancy. Things had happened so quickly, and suddenly this strong, healthy but average sized church was overwhelmed. Many aspects of church life never did quite catch up with what was going on. A fine example was a move from a small gathering place to a warehouse type facility. Two screens were erected to carry the words of songs. Sometimes words appeared on both screens, but often only on one, and occasionally on neither. In the middle of worship one evening, an acetate was placed on the overhead projector on which were written tiny words. My son quipped, 'this is good, Dad, a worship song and an eye test all in the same evening'. But these were humorous, almost insignificant spots on a huge international canvas, painted by John and Carol Arnott and their team. It was impressive.

I returned several times, at John and Carol's invitation, to speak. It was a privilege. Many of my own team leaders visited and were blessed, challenged and changed.

When the Toronto Airport Fellowship was ejected from the Vineyard network, John asked if I would be a pastor to him as he went through all of this. Copies of correspondence between John Wimber and John Arnott, plus others, were passed on to me. He realised that he was at the centre of a storm, and didn't trust his own judgement. He therefore looked to others for a more objective perspective. I am not sure how influential or important my support was to John and Carol at the time. They seemed to be appreciative, but they had plenty more godly, influential and wiser friends than me around them.

Today, neither Pioneer People, nor I have any formal ties with Toronto. There is a network of churches focussed on harvest, from all around the world. These have met, on occasion, as leaders and I have been glad to participate in a small way. But, as John Arnott has said, 'You guys in England are already so networked as apostles and prophets, I'm not sure what this network will add to you.' I suppose he's right. Through events such as March for Jesus (of which I'm a founding member), Spring Harvest (attended by 75,000 people annually) and a wide range of other forums, the smallness of our island has enabled us to relate in depth, and work together.

Whenever John is in the UK he calls me and sometimes visits. The leaders from our network still go and visit, come back blessed, refreshed and challenged. I have many happy memories of people coming to Christ, being filled with the Spirit, or turning away from life-damaging patterns of behaviour and, of course, there are happy memories of humorous incidents.

One of these stands out above all others. It is standard practice, at international conferences, that the host pays for accommodation and food, but not international phone calls, cost of guests, or wine. Across Europe, most charismatic evangelical leaders and church members drink wine: indeed, in some nations, it is a part of their culture. But it remains a huge issue in North America. Divorce and re-marriage, even among church leaders and high profile music ministries, are seen as unfortunate: but if you drink wine, you are in sin. Following the outpouring of the Holy Spirit in Toronto, and after one or two subsequent visits for ministry, I was invited to a conference in Pasadena. Other speakers included Paul Cain, Tommy Tenney, Mahesh Chavda, Mike Bickle, Frank Damazio and John Arnott. Apparently, at one of the Toronto conferences I spoke at, a bottle of wine I had ordered ended up on the Toronto Airport Fellowship church bill. I don't know whether I paid for it in cash, yet they accidentally put it on the bill, or whether I failed to pay for my Californian Chardonnay myself and that's why it was on the bill. Nevertheless, we were now in Pasadena at a pre-conference dinner, and I felt that a glass of wine with the meal might be a problem for some of those present, so I ordered sparkling mineral water. John Arnott noticed this, made a joke of it, and caused quite a reaction.

'You don't drink, do you?' one of the dinner guests enquired.

'There is nothing I can say to you, that will make you any happier than you are now,' I quipped, and carried on with my meal.

'How much do you drink?' my enquirer persisted. I carried on with my meal. 'You only drink wine don't you – none of the other stuff?' my meal continued. Exasperated at my lack of response my enquirer, sitting opposite, made one final attempt. 'You don't drink to get a buzz out of it, do you?' I placed my knife and fork down, and I responded, then placed my hands in the air and shouted out 'Jesus, help me!' It was meant to be a joke, and it raised a few smiles and laughs, but nothing prepared me for what was about to happen. A man ran around the restaurant and placed himself at the head of our table: 'I help you Señor?' I looked up, we all did. And there he was, the wine waiter, with his name badge pinned on the left-hand side of his collar – and his name – Jesus! The whole table fell about with laughter. That story spread around the world. Thank you John!

In a sense, the Toronto connection changed everything. The desire for personal revival grew stronger; corporate revival became both a pleasure and a pain. The conversions that came out of Toronto, the changed lives, the healed relationships, and the large numbers gave us hope.

If you live in hope – you live in pain!

Chapter Two

The issue coming out of the 'Toronto Blessing' is fairly simple. It is not how much we shake or fall down that matters (though I have done both), but who and what we shake when we get up!

As for the impact on me, the Toronto experience of the Holy Spirit created a sharp focus, and a passionate fire for revival. It has to be said that revival is not what we need. Revival is what we must have to get what we need, which is for every man, woman and child to be able to hear, see and experience the gospel over and over again. And in the so-called 'first world' (the West and North America), that will never happen without revival.

But the 'Toronto Blessing' or the 'Father's Blessing' as John Arnott prefers it to be called, rocketed churches and personalities into the national arena here in the UK. The national press, mainstream television and radio, questioned the nature of church and Christianity for months: so the impact was considerable. Whilst I had already been written about in the national press and had done a little mainstream television and BBC radio, this was different. Conflict is the essence of drama, and the 'Toronto Blessing' brought conflict between conservative and charismatic/Pentecostal evangelicals. Further conflict emerged between traditional/liberal sections of the church and us, and the media played on this. The Evangelical Alliance, a body linking thousands of evangelical churches and ministries, created several forums for theological debate. At one, several Calvinistic, reformed, conservative evangelicals were putting forward a presentation of their interpretation of scripture to criticise Toronto. They drew on the history of revivalists; they sounded authoritative, authentic and convinced. Unfortunately for them, one of the leading revival historians, Professor Tudur Jones, was sitting in the room. Obviously, having heard it all before, he reacted with: 'Rubbish – you don't know your history'. This was all the more amazing as he himself was neither charismatic nor Pentecostal in experience, and neither was he in a church identified with either. The conservative evangelicals asked for more time to put their case, which was about as moving as Emelda Marcos asking for another pair of shoes!

Nevertheless, the presence of conservative evangelicals challenged us, appropriately, to 'search the scriptures', to ensure that we were not on a careless joyride, leading to disaster.

Numerous leading conservative evangelicals, intrigued by what was going on, attended leaders meetings and conferences and found themselves baptised in the Spirit and speaking in tongues! One leading Anglican on the Synod, the governing body of the Church of England, asked for prayer. As I prayed for him, he slid down the wall and collapsed in a heap. London Bible College students asked if I would come and pray for them. I drew from scripture, revival history, and offered to pray with people. Bodies of faculty members and students littered the floor, including one or two who 'didn't believe all this'.

An invitation then came from a leading group of charismatic Roman Catholics. I arrived at one of their colleges to find the theatre was jammed packed: so packed it was dangerous. The stage, the aisles: everywhere was filled. I taught from the scriptures, shared a little of historic revival and contemporary revival around the world, and then gave an appeal. Somebody may as well have shouted out 'Fire! Fire! Fire!' as a stampede began. The Pope's advisor on all things charismatic, and his wife, asked for prayer, and ended up within seconds on the floor, seemingly semi-conscious. Nuns, priests, students and church members were weeping, confessing sin and praying with each other, draped over chairs, lying on the floor or across the stage.

The response was similar at one of the first 'Roots' conferences of the Salvation Army. They had been given a prophecy about their future, saying that they should go back to their roots. The speaker who was to speak before me came to the podium and went to speak, but collapsed on the floor in uncontrollable laughter. The conference delegates were obviously both bemused and shocked. This was a young man with a great heart for the poor, marginalised and powerless. He doesn't go in for a lot of 'churchy' stuff, especially this type of thing. Eventually, I approached the podium, as he was unable to continue any longer, and then we opened the meeting up for prayer. There were literally scores and scores of bodies all across the floor, many in tears, confessing sins, both to myself and to others in the room.

So, having a heart for revival, and having been to Toronto on several occasions, I was drawn-on by the Salvation Army, Roman Catholics, Anglicans, Baptists, the 'new-church movement', YWAM and several other ministries to spread the 'fire'.

As for me, in terms of manifestations of the Holy Spirit or reactions to His presence, very little appeared to happen. On several occasions, whilst in some fairly boring meetings, I found myself laughing on the inside, uncontrollably, with tears streaming down my face. There was no natural reason for this: it had not happened before. I would also find myself weeping when speaking of revival and our nation in meetings large and small.

So, the impact was huge. Whether it was the mainstream denominations I have referred to, or the embrace of the 'Father's Blessing' by the new-church movement (apostolically-linked charismatic churches), or many of the so-called para-church organisations: Toronto, the Holy Spirit and revival were the main topic of discussion for at least two or three years. Mainstream TV carried reports of the 'Blessing' on prime time news and in documentaries.

But there still remain several significant events that have

affected me personally. In the autumn of 1994, several months after the outbreak in Toronto, we erected a huge marquee. Night after night, people came to worship, to listen and to be prayed for. One night, as we were worshipping, the keyboard player could not touch the keyboard, it was almost as though there were some force hindering him from touching the keys and he fell to the ground. This provoked Holy laughter, as I asked for another pianist to help. In jocular fashion, he strode to the keyboard on stage, and found as he put his fingers down towards the keyboards that they stopped about six inches above the black and white keys, and he just fell about with laughter. A theologian friend of mine, who happened to be on the platform, was rolling around the stage and the whole tent was full of laughter. At the end of the month, John Wimber came to speak and we must have had around 1,000 people present. After strong worship and good teaching, he began to point people out in the crowd and pray for them without moving from the platform. The scenes of people jumping up and down 'on fire' falling to the floor, laughing, and crying, made me wonder why Toronto Airport Fellowship had been unceremoniously ejected from the Vineyard network. The tent in Cobham, Surrey, twenty miles south west of Westminster, was just like Toronto.

A friend of mine worked for the Romanian Royal Family. Whilst speaking at a YWAM conference in Switzerland, my friend arranged an audience for me with the King and Queen. Events took place that day, which opened them up to prayer, leaving the Queen in tears. I left her two books, my own autobiography *An Intelligent Fire*,[1] left primarily to let her know where David Taylor, my friend and their employee, comes into the story and another one, by Ravi Zacharias, on the nature of Atheism.[2] I thought the latter would appeal to them as they had been ejected from Romania by the communists fifty years previously. Within a short while, I was told that Queen Anne of Romania wanted to see me. Within days she was in my home, she talked a great deal about the European Royal Family and the need of prayer. What I asked her was, why she had flown from Switzerland to see me, and she replied, 'Because I have read your book. Twice! I thought Christianity was about rules and dogma, but reading your book, I realised that Jesus Christ is looking for friendship with people like me.' We prayed together, and during that time she had a genuine experience of the Holy Spirit and made it clear that she wanted to live every day of her life for Christ. Subsequently, she attended and took part in several meetings where I was speaking. The first was in Bristol. Several hundred gathered for an evening of worship and teaching. During the course of my teaching, I introduced Queen Anne to a startled congregation and she shared her story. Explaining that how, as a result of this recent experience, she had forgiven the communists for all they had done to her husband, in excluding him from the country and what they had done to her people. As she was talking, she was slowing falling backwards. There are two things you do not do with Royalty, the first is you do not touch them, and the second is to raise issues: you are only there to respond to the issues they raise. But, realising what was happening, I put my hand to her back to steady her: I said nothing.

A few nights later the same thing happened, and it was very visible as the congregation was on all three sides of the stage. However, at supper I half apologised for placing my hand behind her back, but said I was concerned for her safety. She then asked me what this was, claiming that on the first night that she told her story she was nervous and put the 'falling' down to that. 'But,' she continued, 'this evening I was fine; I was really enjoying myself, so what do you think this is?'

I hesitated, but responded, 'Well Ma'am, the Holy Spirit is coming to the earth, and people are reacting to His presence even though they cannot see Him. I think this is what was happening to you, even though you didn't know it'.

She paused: 'So this is the Holy Spirit?'

I smiled, 'Yes, Ma'am, I think this is the Holy Spirit'.

There was now a long pause, she broke into a smile and responded, 'Isn't He marvellous!' She has subsequently gossiped the Gospel across parts of the European Royal Family.

There were two other significant events that must be mentioned. In the spring of 1997, one of my advisers told me, 'It's time to dream again'. I had heard that a Chinese pastor had taken an ex-Christian Scientist Church building and was going to turn it into a centre for charismatic evangelicalism. By June, we were meeting five nights a week, several hundred were attending each night, and there was a strong emphasis on worship, the presence of God, repentance and confession. One night, a young man brought five large boxes of pornography to the meeting and placed them at the front. He wanted to give his story publicly and explained how he had purchased one gay pornographic magazine and this had now grown to five boxes of videos and magazines. When asked why he wanted to do this at the Emmanuel Centre, Marsham Street, Westminster, he responded: 'I have sinned for so long in private, I must repent in public', and threw himself across the boxes weeping. We filled a dustbin two or three times over with weapons, drugs, pornography and a wide range of other items: some, apparently harmless, but, nevertheless, addictive, including cigarettes, TV listings, wine bottles and videos.

The meetings carried on in one form or another throughout 1997, and into the spring of 1998. During that time, over 75,000 people came through the doors, with thousands responding in repentance and hundreds giving their lives to Christ for the first time. Marriages were restored, and one couple, who had been divorced because of the husband's immorality, was re-married the following summer. They are still together to this day.

My friend, Noel Richards, had been deeply touched in the Pioneer Network Ministries Forum of May 1994. His trance-like reaction was so uncharacteristic that his wife and friends laughed for days. They couldn't believe it: Noel is always very much in control of his affections and emotions. Certainly, I had never seen anything like it. But he carried a burden to see stadiums filled with worshippers and this experience was a factor that eventually caused us to hire Wembley Stadium in June of 1997. On that day, around 45,000 people gathered for seven hours of non-stop worship and prayer, and I gave an appeal for those present to get right with God. Hundreds gave their lives to Christ, and many more hundreds found their way back to Christ. We had several letters explaining that the presence of God was so strong that, from the moment they arrived, mid-afternoon, to the time they left, late at night, they neither moved to get food, visit the toilets or for any other reason. They remained standing around the stage, on the centre of the pitch, for seven hours.

So, in the year of AD 2000, Anona and I will celebrate our thirty-fourth year of marriage. With the Holy Spirit's help, we have been able to maintain a good relationship with our three sons, Paul, thirty-one, Simon, twenty-nine (now married), and Jonathan, twenty-two. We now live in Westminster. Paul lives in Cobham, and is very much part of the church Pioneer People, twenty miles south west of our home.

We now have our own Teaching, Training, Prayer and Revival Centre in Farnham, Surrey, twenty miles further south west. Jonathan lives in Westminster during the week and in Farnham, at the centre, at weekends. Politicians, revivalists, musicians and Christian organisations are continually using the centre, and a number of churches use the house for their Alpha weekends, with many coming to faith and being baptised in the Holy Spirit.

I currently host an hour-long TV chat show on the Dream Channel, which is broadcast by satellite across most of Europe on a weekly basis. I also take part in a small, fifteen-minute Revival Update, for London's Premier Radio, which is broadcast each week. Both BBC 1 and ITV, our main commercial stations, have involved me in a wide range of programmes including, recently, three one-hour, mainstream, non-religious documentaries on issues of prayer, faith, and behaviour. All of these, in some way, have been affected or influenced by Toronto.

As a result of God's favour, and the blessing that emanated from Toronto, I have been invited to cities in the USA, Mexico, South Africa, Canada, Spain, Germany, Norway, Italy and all across the UK. I have spoken to at least half a million different people face to face, apart from the TV and radio programmes. In one sense, I wish I could leave the story there – Marriage and family strengthened, Pioneer People (our church) doubled in number, our Pioneer network of churches grown considerably, and my ministry, with opportunities to affect 'movers and shakers' and many other people, rocketed beyond recognition of where I was pre-1994 – but this isn't the whole story.

Those six years have been, as you can well imagine, the most demanding, but fulfilling, of my entire ministry. They have also been the most painful. I suppose we come back to the understanding that, 'if we live in hope, we also live in pain'. Hopes for the family, for the church, for the Pioneer network, but more importantly for the nation, were high – perhaps too high. But I'm not a man who wants to live up to my own low expectations of myself.

One cannot help but rejoice at the fact that over 6,000 prisoners have come to Christ since the summer of 1994, as a direct result of the blessing that has come out of Toronto. In the last ten years, at least 10,000 gypsies have also given their lives to Christ, though there is nothing obvious to link that gypsy revival with Toronto. Significant individuals, some I have already told you about, have also come to Christ in that period, but it has not affected the nation as a whole: it has affected the closed communities of gypsies, prisons, small elite circles and, in parts, the black community.

If you are like me, you like to think that life is either all blessing or all problems – but that is not how life is. Blessing, transformation and personal revival are because of the rain that God has sent from Heaven. What we are often not prepared for is that alongside the good springs up the bad. There were things I discovered about myself, at the age of 50, that previously I had been blind to. I had hurt others, and the realisation of that was a painful experience. And alongside the carrots and corn in our church, Pioneer People, emerged more thorns and thistles than I care to mention. While some quality people were being added to us through salvation, or simply because they were attracted to the presence of the Holy Spirit at the church, others were leaving. Within the Pioneer network of churches and training programmes there was undoubted blessing and favour on so many initiatives, but in some churches, changes of leadership were not handled well. As a result of the blessing, several leaders started a much wider ministry and again the transition from the local church was difficult and hurtful.

Again, with high expectations, particularly of our church, we found we neither had the gifting or the wisdom to live up to our own high expectations. Externally, all people could see was that we had the largest church in the area; significant Ephesians 4 ministries drawn to us; our travelling the nation and the nations; and media profile probably unparalleled, with the exception of Holy Trinity Brompton and the *Alpha Courses*. But amidst the profile, blessing, growth and influence, which have come out of the blessings of the Holy Spirit, it would be remiss not to mention the pain that has come out of our hopes for ourselves and for our nation.

I suppose the only hope, from God's point of view, is that there will be people who will live beyond self-fulfilment, blessing, growth and influence, but will also live with the pain that comes with the eternal hope. Our ultimate hope is in Christ, and the resurrection and the age to come. Between now and then, we need more of the Holy Spirit, not less, and more pain to help us handle the blessing with humility and respect for the grace of God.

I can do no better than finish with the words of the writer to the Hebrews: 'Let us hold fast the confession of our hope without wavering, for He who promised is faithful. And let us consider one another in order to stir up love and good works, not forsaking the assembling of ourselves together, as is the manner of some, but exhorting one another, and so much the more as you see the Day approaching' (Hebrews 10:23-25).

NOTES

[1]*An Intelligent Fire*, Gerald Coates, Kingsway
[2]*A Shattered Visage*, Ravi Zacharias, Wolgermuth & Hyatt

DAVID CAMPBELL

David is the Senior Pastor at City Church in St Albans, Hertfordshire, and has been for thirteen years. He is married to Mandy, and they have two daughters, Sophie and Amy. David has been used extensively by God over the last few years to spread the renewing work of the Holy Sprit to many churches in the area. Ministry to leaders is a major passion, and David has forged strong links with other Pastors in the helping prepare the ground for a major move of God. Another passion is Revival and currently, he is promoting this by spearheading 'Prayer for Revival' meetings along with another local leader.

DAVID CAMPBELL

Chapter One

St Albans is a wonderful city to minister in. There is a rich history of Christian witness reaching back to the execution, here, of Britain's first Christian martyr, Alban, in around AD 250. There is also a great sense of working together for the Kingdom, with more than a dozen 'charismatically flavoured' churches in the city. I have been involved in praying for revival with a group of city leaders for fifteen years now. It was at one such prayer meeting, in February 1994, that I first heard of the intriguing events that were unrolling in Toronto.

Bob Craine was a regular visitor to our local Vineyard fellowship and was brought along to our regular Friday morning prayer meeting by its leader, Chris Lane. He had just been to Toronto, and he spoke of how God was moving in amazing power there, and of the way in which there seemed to be something contagious about it. This sounded just what I had always wanted: a 'transferable anointing'! The stories he told, of people being 'stuck to the floor' and experiencing such joy in the Lord that they laughed aloud for hours, were both challenging and appealing to me. I trusted Bob, as he was not a man easily swayed by the 'flavour of the month' and, somehow, I just knew this was God, even before my brain had the chance to analyse it.

I have never been one to fly all over the world, either to conferences or to preach, preferring to see the UK as my mission field: so the desire to jump on a plane and going to Toronto was unusual for me. I shared my first impressions with Grahame Wells, the other main leader in our church, and when he encouraged me to go as soon as possible, I replied that I'd only go if he went with me.

Grahame and I tried our best to get to Toronto as soon as possible but, frustratingly, could not find the time until June, over three months away. However, the wait was well worth it. In the meantime, I spent a day praying with two friends, Colin Dye and Grenville Barber, and they gave me prophetic words saying that the visit to Toronto would significantly change both my ministry and our church. Keith Taplin, who exercises a prophetic ministry in our church, prophesied that God was about to visit our church in such a way that we would not be able to end meetings and that He would disrupt what we considered to be the order of our church. You can't say we weren't warned!

The other leaders in the church agreed with the idea of sending us to Toronto and paid for our tickets and accommodation. Since then, I have seen many churches blessed because they have had the vision to send their leaders (and wives) to centres of outpouring such as Toronto, Pensacola or Argentina, and I would encourage all church leadership teams to consider sending their leaders to 'catch the fire', whether at Toronto, Willow Creek, Pensacola, South America or Korea.

We arrived in Toronto on a sunny June afternoon, in plenty of time for the evening meeting. We dropped our cases off at the 'Hotel Monte Carlo' and made for the hall. Coming from a church that has met in a variety of halls, from schools to hotels, I was quite at home at the Toronto church's industrial unit facility. If anything, I was envious of it: at least this was clean, warm and their own.

I don't know what I expected to find at the Toronto Airport Vineyard Fellowship (as it was called then), but I do know that I went prepared for almost anything. Bob Craine's introduction had prepared me somewhat, and I suppose my Pentecostal background meant that I had heard stories of extraordinary things in past moves of the Spirit. What I was certain of was that I was hungry for more of God and desperate to see His power: firstly in my own life, then in my family, our church and for revival in our city.

John Arnott, pastor of the Toronto Airport Fellowship, was not there that week and we had just missed 'the Bishop', David Pytches, from St Andrew's, Chorleywood, who had left for the airport to return to the UK minutes before we arrived in the hall. Almost everybody who heard our British accents wanted to tell us about the roaring bishop: how David had gone around roaring like a lion all that afternoon. Interestingly, in later days, the whole arena of 'animal noises' became contentious, and Toronto speakers found themselves having to defend the actions of others. My understanding was that less than 1% of attendees at Toronto made what could be described as animal noises, and that 90% of those were British!

Val Dodd, one of the elders, spoke and challenged men who wanted to go on with God to come to the front. Grahame and I almost ran out to the front together. Then Val said, 'turn to face the door on my right, go through into the next room, get yourselves in groups of four or five and confess your sins to each other'. That was not what I expected.

'You go in a different group to me,' I whispered to Grahame. My group finally sat down, and I was desperately trying to think of something small to confess, when one of the men asked if he could go first. The rest of us seemed relieved. He went on to confess that, although he was a leader of a church, he was addicted to pornography and asked for prayer, which we duly did.

Another brother confessed that he was a closet homosexual, who frequented gay bars whilst supposedly attending Christian conferences. By then, I was trying to think of something *big* to confess! So, my introduction to Toronto was firmly rooted in an encounter of freeing holiness and refreshing honesty.

Meetings at Toronto have never been short and, although they began at 7.30 p.m., I never left the hall before 1.30 a.m. on any night of my visit. Ian Ross, and a small faithful ministry team, stayed late every night, praying quietly over all who cared to stay: soaking us with prayer and asking the Lord to come upon us more and more. This 'soaking' up the presence of God was quite new to me, and yet, seemed so obviously a good thing. I was used to the 'quick touch on the head accompanied by a loud prayer' approach to ministry, and this more gentle, but powerful, approach greatly enhanced my appreciation of intimacy with the Father. Since there were no daytime meetings, daytimes were spent either sightseeing or sitting praying and reading the scriptures. It was a delightful surprise, for this ignorant Scotsman, to find that Niagara Falls was only about an hour away, and so we were able to see for ourselves that impressive torrent of fresh water that figured so powerfully in Marc Dupont's prophecy about the well that God was opening up in Toronto. It was a great relief to be away from the telephone and constant interruptions of church life. I suspect that 'getting away from it all' was a key factor in many of us receiving so much at Toronto. The whole focus was on receiving from the Father; soaking up His presence – and that was what we did – for hours on end.

On the second or third evening, I was standing alone waiting to be prayed for, when I heard a voice ask, 'Can I pray for you?' I turned around and, at first, saw no one, but then realised that I had almost poked out the eye of a sweet little old lady from the ministry team. My heart sank, as I realised that, secretly, I wanted a leader to pray for me! I smiled at the lady as, inwardly, I tried to repent of such a wicked sentiment. She went on to tell me that she had not prayed for anyone before this 'blessing' had hit the church, just over four months previously. (This did nothing for my unworthy feelings, but I still smiled.) She went on to say: 'But you are a Pastor.' I was flabbergasted: how did she know? Could it be that I had a 'Ready-Brek' type glow around me? She went on to explain: 'You see, they're the hardest to pray for!' I had seldom fallen over when prayed for in the past (despite receiving prayer from some who had hit me so hard that I was almost concussed), but those words had the effect of draining all my strength away and I hit the floor like a ton of bricks.

As I lay there, I was aware of someone close by laughing like a quiet version of Blackpool Pleasure Beach's Laughing Policeman. Then the embarrassing reality of it struck me, it was me who was laughing! And laugh I did for almost an hour: an hour filled with a sense of well-being with God and an awareness of the intimacy of His love. Some have asked me whether I could have got up from there. My only response is to ask, 'Why would I want to?'

I did not lose consciousness at any point, but was wonderfully aware of waves of the Holy Spirit's presence wafting over me. Although I believe in the sovereign workings of God, I am very aware that, in most cases, receiving is a choice. I made a choice to chase after God until He caught me.[1] Later, I watched with approving amusement, as groups of people tried to get up from the floor, only to briefly meet someone else's eye with the subsequent effect of falling back onto the floor in convulsive and contagious laughter.

I learned a long time ago that God does not limit Himself to my preferences, and certainly, will not indulge my prejudices. I was therefore not surprised to see and hear things that challenged my idea of what is 'decent and in order'. One thing I have discovered, in twenty-five years of ministry, is that God is God, and that gives Him the right to do whatever He wants, whenever He wants, with whoever He wants, and however He wants, without first seeking either my opinion or my permission.

At that point, I had no idea how much this would affect my ministry or City Church, St Albans. All I really cared about was that I had discovered a new level of intimacy with the Father. Many of the folks I met at Toronto told me that they had travelled for miles to be there because they were desperate, burnt-out and on the verge of resigning from the ministry. That wasn't my situation at all: far from it. I was in a great church, full of people I loved and who loved me, seeing growth and reaching out to the neighbourhood. My marriage was in a good place. My wife, Mandy, had encouraged me to take this trip in June, despite it meaning that I was away for her birthday. Everything was good.

Too good maybe? I needed to fall in love with Jesus all over again and learn to hunger and thirst after Him more.

Like Charlie Brown said, 'Everyone wants to change humanity, but no one wants to change himself.' My overwhelming sense, in Toronto, was of being in a hall full of people who wanted to change and be changed. I did not get the sense of being surrounded by hordes of people who were chasing some self-indulgent mystical experience: far from it. One could almost taste the hunger. Personally, I love being with hungry people: those who hunger and thirst after God 'as the deer pants for the water brooks'.[2] Some are so cautious that they never accomplish anything. To mix metaphors, they are so busy being careful not to jump on the bandwagon, that they miss the boat.

Each night, a clear appeal for salvation was given and I was thrilled to see genuine responses every time, even though the great majority of 'pilgrims' seemed to be Christians already: indeed, a high percentage seemed to be church leaders.

The worship was typical of the Vineyard churches: good quality musicians with a bias toward songs that expressed intimacy with the Father. Even during the worship, people were being overcome by the Spirit. Some just fell over, others 'yelped', and still more laughed. By the time the preacher got up, there was often so much noise that it could be difficult to hear what was being said. As someone brought up with a healthy respect for the preached 'Word', this was a stretching experience for me. I later asked some of the folks who had been making such a commotion what was happening to them that caused them to make such a noise. Without exception, I found them to be genuine people. The majority of them were more introvert than extrovert: in other words, the people least likely to want to draw attention to themselves. Many of them had life-changing experiences whilst on the floor: some of which related to what was happening in their bodies. For example, one man who had been shaking on the floor all through the service shared how he felt God was shaking him free of chains that bound him.

Although I was not aware, when I left for the airport, of quite how much impact that short week had had on my life, I returned home from that visit radically different. I was not to return to Toronto for over three and a half years. During that time I kept myself informed on what was happening at Toronto, as well as attending meetings in the UK where speakers from Toronto were ministering. In 1995, we hosted a team from the School of Ministry and some of the speakers at City Church, St Albans.

In January 1998, I returned to Toronto, accompanied by my twin brother, Ian, for the Leaders Conference and in time for the fourth anniversary of the outpouring. At first, I was nervous that this could prove an anti-climax compared to my first visit, but I need not have worried.

Things were different. The church had now purchased its own massive facility and my eye was immediately drawn to the lines of tape at the rear of the hall. I'd heard about these lines. 'What a great idea!' I thought. Being six foot three and of 'goodly' proportions, I know that nobody would enjoy having my body come crashing down on top of them. This practical, caring approach to ministry is typical of Toronto Airport Christian Fellowship (as it was now called) and I was pleased to see that this measure of order did nothing to restrict the flow of the river of blessing. I spent many hours on the floor, soaking up the presence of God, either after, or whilst receiving, prayer ministry.

The ministry team were very organised, and I noticed that they had badges that showed their names and a coding system of dots that related to which groups of people they were authorised to pray for. I was aware that below the easy-going surface, there is a great deal of careful and meticulous planning. As any really good musician will tell you, it takes a lot of practice to be able to play spontaneously.

Although we were there to attend a conference and, therefore, did not see the church as closely as on my previous visit, I was challenged by the fact that the church had stayed so fresh and had not allowed themselves to become complacent, as, to an extent, I felt we had. I resolved to dive back into the 'river'.

Before my second visit, I had been seeking the Lord over an

area of my ministry, namely my denominational role as a District Superintendent. I felt that the Lord wanted me to withdraw from that role for a season and concentrate on encouraging leaders in our part of Hertfordshire. One evening, I was standing in line next to my 'identical' twin brother, when John Arnott came and prayed for us. He prayed blessing on Ian, who hit the floor, and simply said to me: 'Go take your county.' Isn't it great that God can tell the difference between twins?

When I returned from Toronto, I withdrew, for a season, from my wider responsibilities and, with the help of my Vineyard friend, Chris Lane, set up a group called 'Hearts for Revival' and organised City Church, St Albans' first regional conference.

In summer 1999, our family, along with our worship leader, Keith Deal, and his family, spent the greater part of our holiday visiting TACF for its *Have Another Drink* conference. It was so good to see my whole family being blessed. My daughters, Sophie and Amy, loved being away from the pressure of being 'the Pastor's kids' and were, visibly and undeniably, touched by the power of God. Once again, I was at a crossroads in ministry and felt the Lord confirm to me that I should allow myself to be nominated to the office of Regional Superintendent within the Elim movement and now serve as a member of the National Leadership Team.

Ever since my first visit to Toronto, I have encouraged Pastors, church boards, church members, youth workers, (basically anyone who will listen to me), to visit TACF. Many have made the journey and none have complained that it was a waste of time or finance. Some went full of scepticism and questions, and returned happier than a cat in a room full of rocking chairs.

John and Carol Arnott have visited our church several times and we value their friendship. Everyone who has ever met John and Carol quickly feel that they are their special friends: such is their capacity to show the loving acceptance and care that the Father has for each one of us.

Even although I now serve on the national leadership of a Pentecostal denomination, City Church, St Albans, is registered as a Partners in Harvest church. This is a source of great personal joy to me as I am so grateful to the folks at TACF for their unstinting graciousness in the way they have poured themselves out for thousands of churches across the nations and I am proud to be associated with them.

NOTES

[1]Tommy Tenney *The God Chasers* ©1998, Destiny Image
[2]Psalm 42:1

Chapter Two

I love John Arnott's quote, 'Our church was praying for revival, just as many of yours are. We realise now we forgot to ask what revival would look like.'[1]

City Church, St Albans, was a nice charismatic church in a predominantly middle-class city. I always thought of it as 'the thinking man's charismatic church'. We danced as we sang, but we could explain everything that we did, and I was (and still am) impressed by the teaching coming out of Willow Creek on 'seeker sensitive meetings'. Now there were bodies everywhere at all the meetings, how could we fit those philosophies together? Some churches felt they had to reject this blessing from the Father, as it was too disruptive to their orderly services and programmes. We were not given the choice; God just turned up at the church and 'took the lid off'.

When we returned from our first visit in 1994, word was already out that something had happened to the leaders at Toronto. Nearly everyone from the church attended our first Sunday service back and were there ready to start on time at 10.30 a.m. (a significant event in itself)! Grahame led the service, while I stood nearby at his side. Whilst the first song was being sung, people started to fall over without even being prayed for. I knew we were in trouble when the overhead projectionist fell over convulsed with laughter: he was a Ph.D. candidate,

studying the effects of mildew on rhododendron bushes. Hardly
the most suggestible of characters!

'Come and explain what's happening!' Grahame hissed to me.

'I don't know what's happening,' I replied honestly, standing
my ground.

'You're paid to know what's happening,' he replied laughing.

I walked to the microphone and, addressing the congregation,
pointed at the increasing pile of bodies with my right hand and
said simply, 'This – this is a move of the Holy Spirit'. Hardly
had I said the words when three rows of, until then, sober
English saints collapsed in a heap of unrestrained joy in the
Lord. That was to be one of the very few times when the preacher was unable to preach, and we were still carrying people out to
their cars at two o'clock in the afternoon.

We heard later that other churches, such as Holy Trinity,
Brompton, were having similar scenes of God-induced disorder
at the same time. But even if we had been the only church in the
UK to embrace this re-ordering of the Holy Spirit, then we
would have done so: so convinced were we of its divine origin
and purpose.

From the beginning, we prayed that God would give us all
'enough to give away'. We knew that this was not just a new
'toy' for the church to play with, but a wonderful empowering of
His people, as a part of preparing us for revival. Some have criticised the Father's blessing as being an excuse for self-indul-
gence. Where this is true, then the blame must be laid fair and
square on the church and their leaders. There is nothing wrong
with the supply; merely with the distribution system.

On one occasion, I was praying; asking the Lord to send
people in to our outreach programme, when I became aware that
I was praying, 'Lord send the people in,' whilst Jesus had said,
'*Go* into all the world and preach the gospel'(italics mine).[2] After
a few minutes of wrestling with this, I felt that the Lord was asking me: 'David, which part of *go* do you not understand?' We
have been a 'going' church ever since.

The explosion of God's presence amongst us was like a

second Pentecost. It thrilled the church, causing us to fall in love with Jesus all over again, and propelled us out into the world in a procession of mission.

In that first year of the 'river' flowing (the term 'river' has been used widely in Renewal circles to signify the fresh flow of the Holy Spirit today in great power and quantity), our church launched five teams out into short-term missions and planted another outreach congregation. Out of a congregation which was then around 200 people, nearly 100 (including teenagers) went to other nations at their own cost to preach the gospel and strengthen the church. That pattern has been repeated every year since then, and we have seen world missions and national revival become major emphases of City Church, St Albans.

Keith Taplin's words have been visibly fulfilled. We found it impossible to end meetings tidily, often having to carry people to their cars at midnight in order to placate the caretaker of our hired hall. One evening he came in and said to me, 'I see you've put the equipment away, but you'll have to do something about the bodies'. Meetings became 'untidy', often lasting four or five hours, with some appearing to be almost stuck to the floor and unable to get up even when they tried. Visitors came from churches all around the area. Most only visited a couple of times, as the anointing appeared to be contagious and they saw the same phenomena in their own churches, on their return. It didn't matter what their denominational background or 'stream' was; they came, were blessed, and took the blessing home.

I still spend a lot of my time ministering in churches of other 'streams', and thoroughly enjoy the fact that Britain is one of the few countries where the streams flow close enough to each other that there is a real possibility that we can see a river emerge.

One of the major changes I first noticed in the church was that we all got a lot better at receiving, when we were prayed for. There was an expectancy that we would connect with God during ministry times. Hours flew past, as people were ministered to by the Lord. As a busy pastor, I was amazed to find that hardly anyone needed to come for counselling: they were receiving so much direct from the Lord. Often, individuals would stand for long periods of time with their eyes closed, hands held out in front of them bathing in His presence. There was a lot of laughter, as well as tears. Long-standing emotional problems were ministered to and, in general, the Body became healthier.

It didn't seem to matter who did the praying, we connected with the Father direct. Personally, I found the absence of any 'personality cult' refreshing. In a few meetings, we had the children pray for the adults. They tended to pray in packs of three, and we saw amazing things happen. I suppose they had an advantage over us, in that they didn't have to make a special effort in order to 'come as little children'.

We saw much evidence of the Father's heart, with people establishing a genuine love affair with Him. As evangelicals, we were very much in love with Jesus, and as Pentecostals, we enjoyed an experience of the Holy Spirit. Now the Father became much more real in our experience.

I noticed that words of knowledge became much more frequent (and accurate), as I prayed for people, not just in City Church, St Albans, but everywhere I went. However, I was under no illusions; I realised that the anointing makes us all look good; I was merely seeing the Father do more through me than before. I was to see similar things happening all over the country, as I toured many Elim churches. Some churches were totally transformed and continue 'in the river' today, whilst others were affected for a short period of time, before returning to the security of how things were done before. My limited experience would suggest that much, if not all, depends on the heart of the leadership. If they have a settling mentality, they will move on for a season and slow down, whereas, if they have a pioneering spirit they will build the blessing into their church's gene pool and continue to press in for all that God has for them. Revival – not blessing – is our heart's cry.

Soon, we had trained up a large ministry team of people competent to pray for others. This is one of the most enduring changes that took place in our church. We were all released to be dispensers of His grace. Young and old, alike, now minister effectively, and out of a congregation of around 300, we have more than 80 people regularly involved as members of our ministry team. In some ways, there appears to be less of the manifestations in our meetings today, but it would be a mistake to think that the power has been dissipated: rather it has been disseminated. Often, I look out on our congregation at the end of a service and see groups of people praying for each other and there is scarcely a member of the church who does not feel comfortable praying for people. This releasing of the Body to minister, is a major change, as a result of our exposure to the outpouring in Toronto.

Prayer lasts a lot longer these days, as we spend quality time with each person as a matter of course. I had become used to the 'quick touch on the forehead' approach, and had seen God minister significantly to people in those situations. Now we were saying to the Ministry Team, 'don't finish praying, until you've finished praying'. Just because someone falls over when you pray for him or her does not mean that the ministry is over. In truth, it has possibly just begun. Soaking people in prayer, often without being informed of their specific need, is an extremely effective way of releasing God's power on their lives. Often it seems as though the Holy Spirit comes in waves over people. That is why we encourage those who 'fall over' (overcome by the Spirit) to stay on the floor and allow God to minister to them. Our thinking is that, if you feel someone pushed you over when you were prayed for, you should get up right away and speak to a member of the ministry team. If, on the other hand, you felt that God put you on the floor, then He has done that for a purpose, so stay and receive, yielding to His Presence.

As a church, we had always believed ourselves to be open to the moving of the Holy Spirit, but we were to learn what John Wimber meant when he told us, 'My biggest problem is keeping out of the way and letting God do His stuff'. I have often experienced again, my feelings of that first Sunday back after Toronto. I know that God is moving and I know that He is about to do something, but I don't know what, or even what I should do next. It is both a humbling and a releasing thing to realise that you don't have to be in charge any more, that sometimes the right thing to do to keep control of a meeting, is to take your hand off it and let the Lord do what He wants. That is not to say that I would advocate a 'free for all, anarchy rules here' type of situation, far from it. Rather, I am speaking about creating such a safe environment that God can move without our intervention or obstruction. An environment where we realise the truth that if we ask our Father for more of the Holy Spirit He will not give us a snake, a stone or a scorpion; but more of the Holy Spirit. We must have more faith in God's ability to bless us than the devil's ability to deceive us. Of course, we bring everything to the touchstone of the Word, but His predisposition is to bless us and, at the end of the day, God does not have any bad gifts to give us – only good. Therefore, it is impossible for Him to give us a bad gift when we come in the name of His Son, aware of the anointing of His Spirit.

Our tolerance levels for the unusual were raised very quickly. This was aided by the fact that we knew these people who were making the strange noises, the extraordinary shaking gestures, the raucous laughter and unrestrained weeping. We knew them before the river began to overflow in the church, and we still know them. They are not exhibitionists, who suddenly saw the opportunity to claim centre stage in a demonstration of thinly veiled flesh. They are godly, Christ-loving, Christ-centred, Christ-serving people. Weirdness is not the distinguishing mark of spirit-filled people. Some people are weird, full stop they would indulge in strange behaviour no matter where they were. But, the marks of those most affected by the river that burst forth at Toronto is not weirdness, but a love for God, His Word, His people and a passion for the lost. Certainly, that is our experience.

On odd occasions there were those who would use the freedom in our meetings as an excuse for 'fleshly' behaviour, but they stood out like a sore thumb against the backdrop of so many who were being genuinely touched by the Holy Spirit, so they were easy to spot and deal with. It is harder to confront those who sit in arm-folded judgement, denouncing everything that moves, and contributing nothing of substance themselves. Strangely, many of the questions they hurled in condemnation were the same questions that we were asking ourselves. Questions such as, 'Why are people not totally changed after three hours on the floor?' or 'Should the same people come out for prayer time and time again?' The difference was in the motive for such questioning. One was to further the work that God was doing; the other to end it.

To attempt an abbreviated answer to the questions above: this is not a more powerful experience than salvation, which is the most life-transforming experience in the universe. All our problems did not disappear when we were converted, neither do they when we lay on the floor for a few hours under the anointing of the Holy Spirit. However, we have the opportunity to build the blessing into our lives, and if we will do that rather than just stopping short at enjoying the moment, we will grow as Christians. It's old-fashioned dying to self and living for Christ. As to the same people coming out again and again, we are happy to pray for anyone who will humble themselves to be prayed for. Pastorally, we pick up on those who seem to be having difficulty getting through in a particular area.

Worship has become even more important to us as a time of telling the Lord that we love Him and receiving a deep sense that He loves us. In the last couple of years, we have seen a wonderful outpouring of new songs that more perfectly reflect the move of God among us. I believe that music plays a vital role in the life of the Church, and that musicians must be good receivers of the Father's blessing to be able to minister effectively. The extended ministry times were a challenge to our musicians, as they felt they should keep playing and worshipping over the congregation. This meant they hardly ever had the chance to be prayed for, and could be ministering for hours on end. The introduction of tapes and CD's was so simple, and now we play our own worship tapes in the background during extended ministry times.

I have never felt the least tempted to try and turn the clock back and return the church to the way it was before Toronto. I'm not sure that I can remember what it was like, so all-transforming and absorbed into our way of life has the sweep of the river been. Granted, we never came under attack of the vocal and often scurrilous criticism that was levelled at churches such as Holy Trinity, Brompton, or individuals such as Colin Dye and Ken Gott. Even the Sunday Telegraph reporter, who alluded to our church in a colour supplement, did not actually identify us. We were cosseted in anonymity.

However, our vision was growing all the time. We constantly encouraged one another to reach out and not make the mistake of thinking we had 'arrived'. What we have is wonderful, but we know that there is much more to come.

A key phrase at City Church, St Albans, is, 'The church is not the field'. In other words, the church is not the place of ultimate service. Many want to serve the Lord by doing something in the church, but there will never be enough jobs in the church for everybody to be fully employed. God never intended the church to be the field: rather, it is the workman's hut in the middle of the field where we come for food, fun, recreation and inspiration, before going out into the field to reap the harvest. The world is the field and it is white for harvest.

Even pastoral ministry has the harvest field as its final goal. We seek to bring wholeness to one another so that we can more fully do the work of the Father. I am not sure who first said it (I wish it had been me), but it is true that, 'hurt people hurt people'. We must seek to bring the Body to wholeness whilst at the same time reach out to others.

Another key word for me amidst the blessing is 'hunger'. Perhaps more than anything, the blessing stirred up in me a hunger for God, greater than I had ever thought possible. That was what drove me to Toronto, and it is hunger that drives me to seek His face, constantly pleading for revival. Isaiah teaches us that hunger and thirst are the currency of heaven. He tells us that

those who have no money should 'come, buy and eat'.[3] Hunger
for God is the currency of the Kingdom.

There is no doubt in my mind that the Toronto church reflects
much of the character and make-up of its leaders, John and Carol
Arnott. John is a naturally loving sort of man, who immediately
sets you at ease. His gentle firmness, genuine humility and clear
thinking have influenced all that happens in TACF and kept it
safe from being carried away with its own success. I don't think I
have ever met anyone more alive in the Spirit than Carol Arnott.
Seven years on, her eyes still sparkle with the joy and excitement
of seeing the river overflow. I believe that Carol's role in keeping
the river fresh and full of godly fun, is one of the great-unsung
triumphs of the Father's blessing at Toronto. Ministry couples
would do well to learn from them both.

I don't know how significant it is that John and Carol Arnott
are a naturally pastoral couple and that the Father's blessing has
been so focused on releasing the intimacy and awe of the Father,
whilst the outpouring at Brownsville, which has an evangelist,
Steve Hill, to the fore, has been more aggressive in its manifestation, and spawned a holiness-led evangelistic thrust. Certainly,
the two outpourings do seem to have some of the characteristics
of the main leaders welded to them. I imagine that City Church,
St Albans' manifestation of what God is doing reflects the leaders' characters too. I find that a sobering thought, and it encourages me to be a radical, righteous leader, who is chasing after
God and His purposes.

The lasting impact of Toronto on me, has been to release me
into a new intimacy with the Father, a fresh experience of His
power, and give me a foretaste of revival sufficient to encourage
me to spend the rest of my life seeking God for it to happen. City
Church, St Albans, is one of hundreds of churches committed to
working with others in the Body of Christ to see revival come to
the UK. For City Church, St Albans, the outpouring in Toronto
heralded the best season in our twenty-year history, and confirmed to us the need to work together for city-wide revival.
We have made the choice to place high priority on building

relationships with other churches in the county of Hertfordshire, as well as the wider region, in order to keep encouraging one another to 'keep on keeping on' until we see full-blown revival, resulting in mass conversions and a permanent change to the fabric of our society.

Toronto served to open my eyes to the tangible aspect of God's presence, the accessibility of His face, the power of His hand to empowering His Church to reach the nations with His Gospel.

NOTES

[1] John Arnott, *The Father's Blessing* (p.71) © 1995, Creation House.
[2] Mark 16:15
[3] Isaiah 55:1

MARK STIBBE

Mark *is married to Alie and they have four children. He is the Vicar of St Andrew's Church, Chorleywood, Hertfordshire. He has written twelve books and taught extensively both in the UK and abroad. His particular passion is for a marriage of the Word and Spirit. To that end, Mark is currently co-hosting, together with J John, a 'St Andrew's School of Preaching', designed to equip charismatics to preach and teach more effectively.*

MARK STIBBE

I first heard about what was going on at the Toronto Airport Fellowship in June 1994. I had been experiencing a number of difficulties in the church that I was leading and was close to burn-out. During a telephone call to Bishop David Pytches (in which I was asking for advice about a pastoral problem), he described his recent visit to Toronto and the effect that it had on his church, St Andrew's, Chorleywood. As I listened, something in my heart said, 'This is the Lord's work and *you* need it'. Having heard David's report, I arranged to attend a meeting he was holding at Holy Trinity, Brompton a few weeks later.

So it was that, in July 1994, I, along with about a hundred other leaders, found myself at HTB listening to David's testimony of his recent trip to Toronto. As he described what he had seen and experienced, I found myself becoming more and more desperate for a fresh filling of the Holy Spirit. I had been overworking, and even striving, to see my church grow spiritually and numerically. I was exhausted and close to depression. As I listened, David's words were like manna in the desert. As he finished his talk and invited the Holy Spirit to come, I asked God to heal the wounds of ministry and to revive me. As I did so, I experienced wave upon wave of the Father's love. I fell to the floor, and laughed for the first time in years. All around me, people were doing the same. A few yards away, Ken Gott (now a very dear friend) was lying under the font, clearly receiving a fresh touch of God: in fact, from that moment on, Ken and his wife Lois, along with his church, have never looked back. They have witnessed an extraordinary move of the Holy Spirit in the north east of England.

I came back from that day at HTB different. The sense of striving had gone. Slavery had been replaced by sonship. No longer was I being driven by whips, but drawn by cords of the Father's love. As soon as I returned, I made some difficult decisions that I had been putting off for some time and the church entered a season of growth and peace.

However, it was not until October of the following year, that I eventually went to Toronto to see for myself what the Lord was doing. I had been invited many times to go, and now sensed that the time was right. In my own prayer life, I was experiencing a season of barrenness, of the Father's absence rather than presence. So, I made arrangements to fly out to Toronto on my own, in order to see what the Lord was doing and to experience personal renewal. On a Sunday night in October 1995, I packed my bags and prepared to fly out to the annual *Catch the Fire* conference, held at the Regal Constellation Hotel in Toronto. It was to be a pilgrimage that would change my walk with God in the deepest and most lasting ways.

The night before I left for Toronto was immensely significant for me. A number of trusted members of my church prayed for me in the vestry with the laying on of hands. One of them, a Messianic Jew, prayed that God would touch me in the *kishkas*! I had to ask what that meant. She replied that it was the Hebrew word for 'guts'. She explained that I was too cerebral in my Christian life, and needed to be engaged with God at the level of my heart and my spirit. I accepted the truth of that statement, and joined with her prayer that my Christian walk would be one of the heart as well as the head, of the spirit as well as the soul.

Returning home, I sat at the kitchen table with my wife Alie. I talked with her about the impoverished state of my prayer life and she offered her perspective. She said that there were some unresolved issues to do with my abandonment as a baby, and that these were inhibiting me from experiencing the Father's intimate presence in prayer. She also said that she felt I would receive significant healing in this area, at the hands of someone I trusted, within twenty-four hours of my arrival at the Toronto conference – a statement that turned out to be prophetic.

I flew out to Toronto on my own and, after a few days with some friends in the city, I transferred to the hotel, where I was overwhelmed by a crushing sense of loneliness: which I subsequently identified as separation anxiety. Having been orphaned shortly after my birth, I was particularly vulnerable in situations of isolation. This was no exception. However, I resolved to seek God's healing, and that evening went to the first main session. At the end of the talk I went forward for prayer and a middle aged lady, a member of the Toronto Airport Fellowship's wonderful ministry team, walked up to me and prayed. She put her finger on my heart and prayed, 'Father, minister to the sense of abandonment in this man's life'. She then paused and asked whether that was relevant, whereupon I shared my story of how my twin sister and I had been abandoned as babies and placed in an orphanage in North London for the first seven months of our lives. She continued to pray for me, asking the Father to make up the love deficit in my life. As she did so I started to double up and a howl of pain started to rise up from my guts. I recognised it immediately as anger and grief, particularly towards my natural father, who had walked out on my birth mother before my twin sister and I had been born.

For the next few hours, I lay on the carpet weeping over the loss of having never known my natural father. Every so often, this lady would return and 'soak' me (the phrase used by the leadership in Toronto). John Arnott spoke some words for pastors that exactly described my situation. In essence, they were about the need to forgive those who had abandoned and rejected us. The line that struck me was about a ball and chain around my feet and a golden key in my hand: the golden key being forgiveness. This is exactly the picture I had been given by a

prophetic lady at a conference in Derby earlier that year. She had
prophesied that I was in exactly this kind of bondage, but that
there was a golden key in my hand and I would be set free.

That night, I chose to forgive my natural father for abandoning
me. I spoke words of forgiveness and blessing towards him, and
I spoke them out loud. As I did so, I sensed an overwhelming
experience of my heavenly Father's love for me personally. I
struggled to my hotel bedroom, barely able to walk. For the first
time in my life, I felt secure in being all alone: knowing the
Father was sufficient, from that moment, and has been ever
since. My security, significance and self-worth are in Him, not in
my circumstances or earthly relationships. I had received the
Father's blessing and, since that day, I have never looked back.

If I were to identify the single most powerful characteristic of
the Toronto Blessing (as the British media dubbed it), I would
say this: what the Father poured out on the fellowship in Toronto
was the spirit of adoption. More than anything else, I believe the
Toronto phenomenon has been about the lavish, extravagant love
of God, which restores intimacy and joy.

But this was not the only thing I benefited from, as I set my
heart on pilgrimage, in October 1995. It was the Holy Spirit who
was at work in Toronto. As such, there were other characteristic
signs of His ministry, besides this extraordinary eruption of the
fire of God's love. The fire that burned in Toronto (and is still
burning), is also the fire of God's judging, convicting and sancti-
fying power. As such, my time in Toronto not only resulted in
profound refreshing, it also produced moments of extreme
purging and refining.

Let me give you one example. I had published a book about
the Toronto phenomenon called *Times of Refreshing*.[1] This was
published before I visited Toronto itself, and was based on what I
had observed in the many churches and friends that had been
impacted by this move of God. The book itself had met with
severe criticism from some conservative evangelical leaders,
who felt that I was encouraging a *theologia gloriae* to the detri-
ment of a *theologia crucis*. In other words, they felt that I was

not only mishandling Scripture (and was therefore doctrinally unsound), but that I was also encouraging a piety of glory without suffering.

One man had taken a particular dislike to me, and had run a conference a few weeks before my visit to Toronto in which he had publicly described me as a man introducing poison into the church's pot. A friend of mine had attended the conference and had told the man that this was a very unfair representation and had encouraged him to dialogue with me directly, rather than firing broadsides from afar. This resulted in one of the most critical letters I have ever received – a letter full of harsh statements about *Times of Refreshing*, that revealed he had not read it closely and had both misquoted and misrepresented me.

My response was carnal rather than spiritual. I wrote back a long letter railing against his critique and lambasting him for libelling me so publicly, both at the conference he had held and in various other contexts. I then forgot about the matter until, that is, I reached Toronto. On the third night of the conference, I woke up in a sweat. I was on fire from head to toe, but it was not the pleasant fire of God's love, which I had experienced so powerfully a day or so before. It was the fire of God's judgement. It was the power of the Spirit's conviction. I felt totally ashamed at what I had done to this man, so I went to the hotel desk and wrote a letter by hand, begging his forgiveness. Whether I had been right or wrong no longer seemed to matter. I felt like a self-righteous Pharisee and I did not like that feeling one little bit. Later, the man wrote back apologising to me as well.

When you find yourself in a place where the power of God is manifestly present, you not only are encouraged and healed; you also are challenged and changed. What happened to me in Toronto reminded me of a story involving Charles Spurgeon. A friend of Spurgeon called Dr Newman Hall once wrote a book called *Come to Jesus*. Another preacher published an article in a newspaper slandering Hall. Hall took it on the chin for a while. But when the article became increasingly popular, Hall composed a letter of protest. His response was full of clever comments that were far more instructive than the original invective. Before sending the letter, Hall showed it to Spurgeon. Spurgeon read it and told Hall that it was excellent, except that it lacked one thing. Underneath his signature, Spurgeon told Hall to write the words, 'Author of *Come to Jesus*'. The two men looked at each other for a few moments, and then Hall tore his letter into tiny pieces.

In my situation, sadly, I had not torn up my original letter. However, in Toronto the presence of God's holiness had been so strong that I was left in no doubt about the sinfulness of my actions. The Holy Spirit convicted me profoundly, and I saw how my behaviour was utterly inconsistent with the character and teaching of the Lord Jesus. I did the best I could under the circumstances. I could not prevent the letter from being sent, but I could obey the prompting of the Spirit and ask that the man tear it up instead. His reply to me was nothing short of gracious. I thank God for him in my prayers.

In his letter to the Ephesians, the Apostle Paul calls his readers to maintain the unity of the Spirit through the bond of peace. Unity is the passion of the Father, the prayer of the Son, and the work of the Spirit. If there is another abiding memory that I have of my pilgrimage to Toronto, it has to do with unity. In just about every session, the emphasis was on the need for renewed churches to work inter-dependently rather than independently. It was constantly stressed that there can be no revival in a community, a city or a country, until dividing walls have been broken down.

During the conference, I recalled a story about an American flying across the Atlantic to England. It was planting season, and when he looked down and saw the stone fences and the geometric designs in the English countryside, he thought it was so beautiful. He stayed in England for several months. Then, when he flew back to America, back across the same area, the fences were all gone. He asked the flight attendant what had happened to the fences. She said, 'Oh sir, it's harvest time. The wheat is now higher than the fences, so you can't see them.'

This emphasis on unity had a profound impact on me

personally. Shortly after coming home from the conference, I wrote this:

> The Lord showed me in Toronto that I am far too self-sufficient in my relationships with other church leaders. While there, I was very struck by Psalm 133: that God gives His commanded blessing where there is unity between brothers. I was also struck by the realisation that a community will only experience revival when church leaders are united in acceptance, love and prayer. As I saw this, I suddenly understood the extent to which I had isolated myself. That isolation has derived from pride. I have had to face that head on, and ask the Lord for cleansing. One practical consequence of this has been a new desire to get together with other churches and church leaders in my area. A vicar who works very near me was at Toronto during the same conference. He spoke with me on the last day and suggested that we, and other church leaders, should meet in order to pray about hosting conferences in our part of the city. I am really excited about this possibility and now want to give time to that. I believe the Lord will pour out a very strong anointing when those of us in leadership repent of our individualism and start to unite in prayer.

I am happy to report that the neighbouring minister in the city where I was working at the time took the initiative to gather leaders to form relationships and pray. This was the beginning of a new level of unity in that part of the city. It has resulted in many meetings and conferences that have brought renewal and hope in a very barren part of our nation.

I constantly thank the Lord for what He has been doing in and through the Toronto Airport Fellowship, from 1994 onwards. I am well aware of the criticisms of what has happened. Some of these are, undoubtedly, fair – others are not. However, the Bible encourages us to judge a work by its fruits not its roots. I am happy to report that the ministry of the people of Toronto Airport Fellowship has been immeasurably fruitful. Millions have visited the church and been totally transformed by the power of God in that place. My own life is testimony to this fact.

I remember one man I tried to counsel when I arrived as the

new Vicar of St Andrew's, Chorleywood (replacing Bishop
David Pytches). He had been a missionary for decades and had
never experienced intimacy with God. His whole Christian life
had been lived with a sense of God's remoteness, rather than
nearness. He had never, at any time, felt the power of God's
Spirit in an experiential and tangible way. As such, his relationship with God, his wife and his people had been, for the most
part, cold and distant. I tried to get to the root of his problems
(much of which centred on his father). In the end, I recognised
that the only way a breakthrough could come would be by divine
revelation and intervention. I shared my own story of how the
Father had healed me in Toronto, and then recommended he
attended the *Catch the Fire* conference in 1998. He raised the
money, booked his place, went to the conference, and was profoundly healed. He came back a different man and, ever since,
has been sharing his testimony of the Father's love. He is a real
encouragement and blessing to his family, his church fellowship,
and to all who meet him. Only the Holy Spirit can do that!

The work continues in Toronto. The emphasis in the church is
now on reaching the city, through strategic evangelism, as well
as refreshing believers from all over the world. I went back there
in March 2000 with my friend J. John and two of his staff, and
we were all richly blessed and refreshed by the rich sense of
God's presence in the church and its ministry. Indeed, one of our
number experienced the power of God for the very first time
(and in a most dramatic way).

John and Carol Arnott are wonderful people, with generous
hearts. They just love giving away what they have received and
it is always a joy to meet up with them when they come to the
UK. They are always hungry and thirsty for 'More, Lord!' Their
stories of what the Holy Spirit is doing never cease to put a new
passion for the Kingdom in my heart, and in the hearts of many
others. They have been regular visitors to Chorleywood and to St
Albans in the last two or three years, as have other leaders associated with the past and present work in Toronto (such as Marc
Dupont). Though some people have found certain manifestations

very difficult, few doubt the integrity of John and Carol Arnott, and I know of only a very few who would question whether their ministry has been of God.

Churches throughout the world owe a huge debt to the Arnotts and their people, for the sacrificial way in which they have hosted a move that has indeed been the Father's blessing to the nations.

NOTES

[1]*Times of Refreshing*, Mark Stibbe (Marshall Pickering/ HarperCollins Religious)

DAVID DALLEY

David *has been an elder at Bath City Church since 1991.*
He is a gifted Bible teacher, with a well-loved inspirational
and humorous style. David developed a course for new
Christians called 'Power for Living', on which he teaches
foundational truths from the Bible. David is married to
Faith and they have three children.

DAVID DALLEY

Chapter One

In 1993, I left my teaching career behind, having agreed to become a full-time elder at Bath City Church. I actually started the new job in January of 1994, and my overwhelming memory of that time is that it all felt like hard work. I had heard rumours of laughter and other happenings at the church in Toronto, and just thought 'Oh, that's nice'. Then over the next few months, I began to hear that this phenomenon was somehow 'infectious': that people would go out to Toronto and then, on their return, would find the same thing happening in their churches at home. Also, inevitably, there was opposition from some quarters to the whole thing.

Some time around May or June, we had a meeting at which the worship just seemed to go on – people wouldn't stop – and I remember thinking how unusual this was. It occurred before we had made any actual contact with Toronto, but there was already a longing for something new in the church. Late in July, Paul Wakely, a fellow elder at Bath, and I discussed what was going on, and concluded that we didn't know what it was, but we knew it was something. So, we agreed that the following Sunday, at the end of the meeting, we would invite people to come to the front if they wanted prayer to receive 'more of God'. That Sunday after-noon, I returned from a trip to Devon, and discovered that, after a powerful morning, Paul had gone to the house of Kim and Jean

Freeborn (at the time, head of Kenneth Copeland Ministries in
Bath), and they were falling about under the power of the Spirit.
The same thing happened again later at another person's house.

The next Sunday, we did the same thing, calling people out for
prayer. I was a bit apprehensive, but basically felt that it would
be good if a few people were to laugh. Well, there were bodies
everywhere; it was mayhem; we prayed for people and they just
fell over. But I began to realise that it wasn't actually affecting
me. To respond to the happenings, we started holding meetings
several times a week, because we had a deep conviction that this
was God: a refreshing move of God. People found the laughter
very releasing, and began to say that they had felt God's presence. I eventually got badly 'drunk' myself and had to be literally carried out, over piles of bodies which littered even the foyer
outside the main meeting hall. We lived, at the time, in a house
that had twenty-eight steps up to the front door! My wife Faith
asked me what I was doing/feeling. I told her I didn't know. I
spent most of the night laughing – getting somehow freed – and
the whole thing 'loosened' me quite a bit. I realised it was alright
to do all these things.

Increasingly, faithful, long-time Christians were having
'encounters' with God, which were both encouraging and
upsetting them. It seemed to arrive in waves: it was like an
infection, a virus. People came from all over the place to our
renewal meetings, and travelled around the country to ones being
held elsewhere. We were also hearing stories of people who
had gone to Toronto and found nothing happened to them
there, but then got back to their home church and started howling
with laughter! If you were religious, obviously, this was extremely offensive. The bottom line, though, was that Paul and I
believed that this was the Lord. Of course, some people did silly
things, but we could see, for instance, that real pain was coming
out.

I considered going to Toronto, but it was already strong and
powerful here in Bath. We did have various visitors from
Toronto come across to us, and I began to realise that they were

bringing a message that this was the Father's blessing: He had come to the church to bless it.

My first visit to Toronto was in 1995. When I walked in, I was immediately overwhelmed by the Father's love: I realised that He *really* loved me. Up until that point, I felt that I had disappointed the Lord many times, but now I just wanted to cry and cry because I knew He loved me. Until then, I had *believed* that He did, intellectually. Indeed, I realised that most of my faith was intellectual, and this process was taking it from head knowledge to my heart. Again, up until then I knew that He was always there, because it said so in His Word! But I never felt Him. I was from an evangelical background, which heavily emphasised that faith was about fact, not feeling: you just believe and stay faithful to the end. So I just felt, 'Oh, what a relief: the Holy Spirit is real!'

I went over for their pastors' training month, which is a kind of mini School of Ministry. It had a devastating effect on me. Not long before I went, a member of our church called Joy Fraser had a clear word from the Lord that we were to 'get ready'. Well, obviously I had been wondering about this. In what way were we to get ready, logistically, I mean? After going to Toronto, I realised that it was our *hearts* that we needed to get ready. I heard the Sandfords' message, about inner healing, lifting judgements off of people, and how powerful that was, how crucial. It dawned on me that in our church there were lots of lovely people, as well as myself, who had made judgements.

I have been to Toronto four times now, and each time it challenges some darkness in me: brings up issues. One time I was in a meeting and someone I didn't know came up to tell me God had given them a word for me. Now, before going, I had reached a point of saying to myself that although I had always loved youth work, I had to accept the fact I was now too old for it. So it was devastating to hear this person tell me from the Lord, 'you have said, "I'm too old for youth work", but that's not what I have said. You and your wife are to be a father and mother to many spiritual children.' Devastating!

The cumulative effect of all these experiences made me realise that God was much bigger than I had realised. I began to think back upon what I had preached in the past, and saw that all my best thoughts had come out of a poverty of experience. When I understood that God is so very merciful, it completely devastated me. Previously, I had thought that I was doing okay: I now realised I had been ignorant, arrogant and proud, thinking I was 'doing God a good turn' by being on His side.

I am still astonished by the numbers from all over the world going to Toronto. They find a gentleness there, a sensitive and very loving leadership. It is a safe place, where you can feel free to speak about your worst sin without feeling condemned. When you are prayed for, it continues to be powerful. There is a sense of the church being more ordered now, and of the intercessory and prophetic coming out. So, our church members were among planeloads of desperately hungry Christians who were flying out to Toronto. We haven't established any formal links with Toronto Airport Christian Fellowship, but have been exceedingly blessed by many of the guys who have come from there to visit us. They all seem very stirred about Bath and what God is doing here.

Chapter Two

Back in Bath, there was also a strong prophetic spirit around, especially in the prayer times at the end of our meetings, in the ministry. We were continually saying 'Holy Spirit, please don't stop! Keep coming', because, apparently, a number of churches in the city had experienced laughter and so on, but then it had petered out. I remember in one meeting, a woman went down in the power of the Spirit who had chronic neck problems and unable to move her head much. Her husband was standing around impatiently, wanting to go home, but she kept saying that she couldn't, that her neck was pinned to the floor. When she finally did get up, it was totally healed.

Before Toronto, I would compare my spiritual life and that of others to a music centre with the volume set to zero, instead of ten. What has happened has allowed the level to reach about four, so far, and even that turns out to be deafening! I think revival, if you like, is when the volume goes up. To use another metaphor, what has happened so far is really just a starter. We aren't even on the main course yet! He is a big God, and He can break out wherever He wants.

Following my clear directive from the Lord, in Toronto, I am again very much involved with the youth in church, which is what I love doing: being there to express love and approval to them. My daughter, Sarah, had a place at university, but wanted to go out to the School of Ministry in Toronto. After that, she stayed on longer, working there in the kitchens, and was eventually asked to help with the administration. Her life is completely different now: she is growing into a powerful woman of God and is very discerning. When we see her, she always prays for us, and she will prophesy over us. She really 'knows things'. She got off to a slow start, but eventually became the class 'drunk', as one of the meeting videos reveals!

We had a word some months ago from a church member called Gillie Horsfall, that God was going to 'pull the rug from under every dependency that was not of Him.' I had always been brought up to believe – indeed had it drummed into me – that I was 'saved to serve'. I now know this is not my primary purpose: I am a human being, not a human doing. We have discovered that God wants a close, intimate relationship with His people, and this provides a safe place to open up and release pain. Experiencing of the father-heart of God has led to an increasing softness of heart in our people. We are becoming more accepting and affirming than we were in the past, and have a wider view of what God is doing in the world.

In the past, I have been guilty of thinking privately about our fellow congregations in the city, 'can any good come out of *that* church?' This proud arrogance is gone, replaced by an increased excitement and longing for revival here. I have repented of this judgement on other ministries in the city, and want friendship. I have discovered that we can love each other and pray for each other, without having to sort out our doctrinal positions first! In the past, I would have been tempted to launch straight into some 'I'm right, you're wrong' diatribe on a theological issue. Instead, I long for God's manifest presence. As I look around the church, I see that people are more in love with Jesus than ever. That has to be a good effect. God enjoys fun, and this really should not be a surprise to us. Doesn't any father enjoy having fun with his kids? We've also learned that church is not about having a big-shot in the pulpit, but that it is God's intention for the whole body to come alive, as set out in Ephesians 4. It's so exciting.

On the downside, we are definitely viewed as being on the radical edge of what is acceptable, within the city. Within our own body, people have had real questions and we have tried to be open and honest. One doctrine a lot of people have grown up with is, 'The Bible says that I am a new creature in Christ, the old has gone and the new is come', and I think this is a barrier for some to accepting the need for inner healing because it ignores the biblical process of being transformed into His image.

For the future, I am expecting to see the glory of God manifested in Bath and revival to come. I am expecting that the reality of the spiritual warfare in which we are engaged will become more real. A city can change, and the rule of God can come. We have seen something of this in a video entitled *Transformation*, about a city in South America. Marriages will be restored; children's hearts will turn back to their fathers and vice versa. The Bride will be made ready. We will see power wielded in a good and godly way. Personally, I am expecting the return of Jesus, but we should live as if that will be tomorrow, and plan as if it is not for another hundred years.

R.T. KENDALL

R.T. *is married to Louise. They have two grown-up children, T.R., who is married to Annette, and Melissa. R.T. has been minister of Westminster Chapel, London for twenty-four years. He is the author of several books and preaches at conferences all over the world.*

R. T. KENDALL

I remember it as though it were yesterday. Lyndon Bowring, Executive Chairman of CARE Trust (Christian Action Research and Education), Charlie Colchester, Executive Director of CARE and former churchwarden of Holy Trinity Church, Brompton, and I were sitting at a table in a Chinese restaurant in Soho, London. As we were waiting for our food to be served, Charlie spoke up: 'Have you guys heard about this Toronto thing?'

Lyndon and I looked at each other quizzically. We hadn't.

Then Charlie continued, 'Well, I don't know where to begin. The oddest thing has been happening at our church at HTB. People are falling on the floor and laughing – I've never seen anything like it in my life'. He continued, 'Last Sunday night, when we left the church at eleven o'clock, there were still about fifty bodies on the floor. I hated to go home and leave them, but we had to. I've never seen anything like it. What do you all think of this?' Charlie told us about a young lady staying with them, who was a graduate of Calvin College, Grand Rapids, Michigan. She had no background of this sort of thing whatsoever, but got involved in the laying on of hands and commented: 'I can't get over it – I just reach out my hands and they fall and they start laughing!' The fact that this girl had been to Calvin College made me think. I know about that College and its background, and for her to be involved in something like this did surprise me

73

a bit. However, if you had put me under a lie detector and asked me if I believed this was of God, I would have had to say, 'no'. Lyndon and I looked at each other and neither of us was very impressed. But Charlie was so excited about it that it left me thinking about it all evening. We left the restaurant to go see the film *Schindler's List*, which was showing in Leicester Square, and then afterwards we went to St Ermin's Hotel and discussed the evening. I found myself thinking more about Toronto than I did *Schindler's List*! I was really taken by what Charlie said, but still did not believe it was of God.

For one thing, I didn't want to believe it was of God, because if God were going to do something great, I felt He would have done it with us at Westminster Chapel first! After all, we had borne the heat of the day; we had paid the price; we had been out on the streets; we had witnessed to tramps, to beggars, to tourists, to anybody. Holy Trinity Church, Brompton is up-market: the congregation is, largely, posh and Anglo-Saxon. Here we were trying to reach all of London. So, I reasoned, if God were going to do something, it would not be in a church like HTB.

In the meantime, I had just had three hundred cards printed up for our new Church Prayer Covenant. One of the petitions of our new Prayer Covenant which was to be introduced in just four or five days from then was: 'We pray for the manifestation of the glory of God in our midst, along with an ever-increasing openness in us to the manner in which God chooses to turn up'. I introduced this the following Sunday and explained the reason for this particular petition. Sometimes God turns up in strange ways. I know a little bit of church history; I know about the Cane Ridge Revival – how strange things happened there. I know that people would fall and sometimes they would laugh and do odd things. This happened again in the Great Awakening in Jonathan Edwards' day and it happened in Whitefield's day. John Wesley criticised Whitefield for allowing this sort of thing to go on, but John Wesley eventually came to accept that you have to put up with these things. So I explained, in unveiling this petition, that we must allow for God's unusual ways. I then used, as an example, what was going on at HTB, but then added, 'I don't happen to believe this *is* of God, but we must be open to the sort of thing God can do'. And so I told everybody publicly that what was going on at HTB was not of God – and I was only trying to be honest.

A couple of days later, a group of ministers were meeting on the premises of the Chapel. I went in to say hello to some of my friends, and there was Lyndon. He introduced me to Bob Cheeseman, who was pastor of a church near Richmond. This man had just returned from Toronto and his face was aglow. I looked at him and asked, 'Tell me more about it.'

He replied, 'All I can tell you is that I've never felt Jesus to be so real in all my life. We have just got back from holiday. Usually I will take a novel on holiday to read, but this time I only wanted to read my Bible. I've never had anything like this happen to me in my life.'

It was the glow on his face that impressed me most, and how he wanted to talk about Jesus. Then I looked at him. I said, 'Look, would you like to come into the vestry and pray for me?'

'Sure, I'd love to,' he replied.

So I said, 'Well, I'm going back into the vestry, and when you've finished out here, come in and pray for me.'

I only remembered that a close friend of mine was coming for coffee as I went back to the vestry, and he was already there waiting for me. I explained to him that somebody who had just returned from Toronto was going to come in and pray for me in a few minutes and added, 'You've heard about this Toronto thing?'

'No,' he replied, 'what do you mean by that?'

'You mean you haven't heard of this Toronto thing? People falling down etc?'

He said that he hadn't.

'Well, I don't think it's really of the Lord,' I continued, 'but I have to say that this guy I just talked to was glowing and so full of joy that I have asked him to come in and pray for me.'

A few moments later Bob Cheeseman knocked on the door, and when he came in he recognised my friend! They knew each other really well. I asked Bob to explain to my friend what had happened to him in Toronto. So he explained to him how he had gone there and was prayed for, blessed, and how it changed his life, and how now it has spread into his church.

Again, I asked Bob to pray for me.

'Well, he can pray for me too if he likes,' said my friend. He had no conditioning for this sort of thing whatsoever. He is a Reformed Baptist preacher, well-known in London and throughout England.

I said, 'Fine.'

But as Bob began to pray, there was a knock on the door, and it was Gerald Coates! Gerald was one of those ministers already present at the meeting on the premises and was simply calling into my vestry to say goodbye. I told Gerald that Bob was about to pray for us and Gerald said that he wanted to be in on it too. So now Bob and Gerald were going to pray for me and, just to be polite and courteous, my friend who happened to be there was going to let them pray for him.

They started praying. In less than a minute my close friend, who had no idea what was going on and had not even heard of this phenomenon until a few minutes before, fell forward, face down on the floor. There he was, before my eyes, flat out on the floor, head down – and I was sobered. I had never had anything sober me like that in years and years.

He lay there for about ten minutes. Finally, he got up, and I asked, 'What happened to you?'

'All I know is, I fell, and I couldn't stop it,' he replied.

He told me later that, for about a week, he had felt an unusual sense of the presence of God unlike anything he had known in years.

Next, they began to pray for me – all three of them! Before they started praying, I took off my glasses because I thought I would be next on the floor! They prayed, but nothing really happened to me – it had happened to my friend instead – but that was the first real turning point in my thinking.

A few days later, I got a phone call from Mr Kenneth Costa,

who is a merchant banker and the present churchwarden of Holy Trinity, Brompton. He called me to see if I had any sermons on 1 John 4:1–3: 'Beloved, do not believe every spirit, but test the spirits, whether they are of God; because many false prophets have gone out into the world. By this you know the Spirit of God: Every spirit that confesses that Jesus Christ has come in the flesh is of God, and every spirit that does not confess that Jesus Christ has come in the flesh is not of God. And this is the *spirit* of the Antichrist, which you have heard was coming, and is now already in the world.'

As it happened, I did have some sermons on this, and he sent a courier across London to pick them up. In the meantime, he asked if I would have lunch with him at the Savoy (no less!) the following Friday, because he wanted to discuss these sermons and get my opinion on what was going on in his church. He was slightly troubled by it, and he seemed to have some trust in me as a Bible theologian. The fact that he turned to me made me naturally appreciative of him and the fact that he was concerned about a text like 1 John 4:1-3 told me that he had not lost his head!

I went to that lunch fully loaded and equipped to explain to him how he must be careful of all this. I was going to persuade him to distance himself from it, although I could not forget what had happened to my friend when he was unexpectedly prayed for and brought to the floor.

During that lunch, Ken began to explain to me what was going on. He said that he himself had been touched. He told me about having to address a group of men, and that as he began to address them he started laughing and could not stop himself: he'd never had anything like that happen in his life. He then expressed the need for sound doctrine, sound teaching and good preaching. He said, 'R.T., your day is coming, because this sort of thing is going to need preaching to undergird it and to make it sound. So be ready!' That, of course, made me think.

Before that luncheon was over, I had a strange feeling that I might have been on the wrong side of the issue. I remembered reading that in Jonathan Edwards' day there were those – supposedly 'sound' – who opposed him. I remembered also that, often, the very ones who opposed what was going on in the Welsh Revival were sound and orthodox. I wondered if I was going to succeed those who opposed Jonathan Edwards and those who opposed Evan Roberts in 1904. I feared that I might be getting on the wrong side, all because of my pride and my anger that this sort of thing could happen at Holy Trinity, Brompton and not at Westminster Chapel. I felt that God had betrayed me and let me down – that we should be the ones to be blessed if God was going to do anything big in London.

It was obvious, by this time, that something *was* happening. Ken Costa is a man of integrity and I knew that he would not defend anything that was not truly of God, and that he only wanted help. So then, it was Ken's integrity, combined with my friend falling on the floor unexpectedly, which made me conclude that I was on the wrong side of the issue.

Later that afternoon, I said to Louise, my wife, 'I think I've been wrong. I have a deep-seated fear that this thing *is* of God'.

'Well, I am interested to hear you say that,' she replied.

I then told her that I believed I was going to have to change.

The following Sunday morning, after wrestling with this for a couple of days, I went into the pulpit and before the morning prayer reminded my people that I had previously made the point that what was going on in various churches, especially Holy Trinity, Brompton, was not of God. I said to them, 'I'm afraid that I was wrong. Today I have to climb down. I believe that what is going on at HTB is of God.' I reminded them of what I had said so many times over the years: 'What if Revival came to All Souls, Langham Place, or Kensington Temple, but not to Westminster Chapel, would we affirm it?' They all knew this had been my theology: that Revival might not come to us, but might come elsewhere. Mind you, I always thought it *would* come to us. But I realised now that God was doing something elsewhere and He had bypassed Westminster Chapel. And by this time, I was beginning to be very, very scared that we could miss it entirely. So I said to the people, 'I believe something has happened: it is of God, it is going on at Holy Trinity, Brompton, and I would not blame anybody if they wanted to go there and investigate it.' Then we bowed our heads and prayed for Holy Trinity, Brompton, and Sandy Millar, their Vicar. On that day I nailed my colours to the mast and, though it had not come to Westminster Chapel, I said, 'It is of God.' Now everybody knew where I stood.

Many people came around and thanked me for my honesty. Some started attending HTB and we lost members as a result. Others fell out with me because I affirmed such a thing. I had one deacon who opposed me for it. He eventually left the Chapel.

A few days later I wrote a letter to Sandy Millar and quoted the verse, 'Come over to Macedonia and help us' (Acts 16:9). I said, 'Please come to Westminster Chapel one evening; I will have all our deacons and wives there, and I'd like you to bring some of your people and pray for each of us.'

He kindly wrote back and agreed to come. We held a buffet supper for the deacons and wives and also for a dozen or so of Sandy's people. He graciously addressed our deacons for about half an hour and then asked us to stand, while he and those who had come with him prayed for various people. Three or four of the deacons and one or two of their wives fell to the floor, but there wasn't a lot of laughter or anything like that. It was, however, a sacred moment. I was prayed for and I felt a heaviness come over me which I could have resisted, but felt that if I did I would regret it as long as I lived. I gave in to it and I too fell forward, face down. I was embarrassed, but I also knew that if I had resisted it with all of my strength, which I think I might have done, I would have felt for the rest of my life that I was too proud to give in. I have never regretted that I gave in to it. On the other hand, I cannot say there was any great joy or laughter, yet it was a matter of obedience to the Holy Spirit.

When the evening was over, because the majority of the men and their wives were largely unaffected, as far as unusual manifestations were concerned, I concluded that we had no mandate to push hard for this sort of thing at Westminster Chapel. Had there been more response, I would have done it, but I felt it would be premature at that time to go into the church and say that we were going to do this too. I believe I took the right decision, and yet I was now publicly identified with the 'Toronto Blessing', as it had come to be called. An article about me appeared in *Renewal Magazine* shortly after that, and so, many in evangelical Britain knew that I identified with the 'Toronto Blessing'. That was in the summer of 1994.

Not a lot happened for a while after that. We went away on our summer holiday to Florida, where I enjoyed fishing in the Keys. I kept in touch with what was going on in London: it seemed that the 'Toronto Blessing' was spreading like wildfire all over London and all over England, but it was not coming to the Chapel. I returned home in September, and decided that I would not do anything to discourage the 'Blessing' from coming to the Chapel, nor would I do anything to work it up or hasten its entrance.

In the meantime, I began to have two fears. The first fear was that the 'Toronto Blessing' would never come to Westminster Chapel and that we would be bypassed altogether. This terrified me. But I had a second fear: that it would come to Westminster Chapel and turn our church upside down, and we'd be back in another grave crisis. I had been through a number of crises in the past and I didn't want another one. Yet, I was prepared for it if this was what God wanted.

In December of that year, 1994, Colin Dye of Kensington Temple asked me if I would like to meet Rodney Howard-Browne. Now all I knew about Rodney Howard-Browne was what I'd seen of him on a famous video. Gerald Coates had invited Louise and I to his home back in July of 1994. Ellie Mumford, the lady who was responsible for bringing the 'Toronto Blessing' to HTB, was there that evening. Her husband is the pastor of a Vineyard church in London. So Gerald, Anona, Ellie, Louise, and I watched this video of Rodney Howard-Browne, which showed him speaking in tongues and laying hands on people. They would start laughing, and doing things that were very unusual, to say the least! This video later became 'Exhibit A' for why the 'Toronto Blessing' must be of the devil but, for some reason, I was not offended by it at all. As a matter of fact, I was even touched and edified by it, and felt that there was something very powerful and of God, because God loves to offend our sophistication. '"For my thoughts are not your thoughts, nor are your ways My ways," says the Lord. "For as the heavens are higher than the earth, so are My ways higher than your ways, and My thoughts than your thoughts"'(Isa. 55:8–9). 'But God has chosen the foolish things of the world to put to shame the wise, and God has chosen the weak things of the world to put to shame the things which are mighty; and the base things of this world and the things which are despised God has chosen, and the things which are not, to bring to nothing the things that are, that no flesh should glory in His presence' (1 Cor. 1:27–29).

I never expected to meet Rodney Howard-Browne, but when Colin Dye asked if I would like to meet him I said, 'Yes, I'd love to'. Lyndon Bowring joined me. Lyndon has had a strange habit of turning up with me at critical moments! Not only was he with me when we first heard about Toronto, but the first time I met Paul Cain I wanted Lyndon to be there. I had heard strange things about Paul Cain as well – that he was occultic and could not be a man of God – but after spending a few moments with him I knew I was wrong about him and felt that I was honoured to be in the presence of such a man of God. And now Lyndon was going to be with me to meet Rodney Howard-Browne.

I remember sitting at the breakfast table at a hotel in Wembley. Rodney was there at the Wembley Conference Centre, where he was preaching every morning and evening that week. I had never seen him in person before but, as I sat across the breakfast table from him, a phrase kept coming to my mind. I could not turn it off. The phrase was: 'Baby Isaac.' Without telling him about this, I recounted to Rodney how, almost exactly two years before, in 1992, I had sat at another table in that very restaurant, putting the final touches to a talk I gave at the Wembley Conference Centre, for the first *Word and Spirit Conference* that Paul Cain and I held. I told Rodney how that night, during the meeting, I had made what I can only call a 'prophetic statement'. It was this: that, just as Abraham sincerely thought that Ishmael was the promised child, and believed that to be so for some thirteen years, in the same way, many people have thought that the Charismatic Movement was the Revival for which everybody was praying. I explained to them that this was not the case. When Ishmael was born, Abraham and Sarah had believed that this was God's way of fulfilling His promise, but it had a natural explanation – there was nothing supernatural about Ishmael, but there certainly was with Isaac. I told the people that God wanted to do something in His church that defied a natural explanation. So many things that happened under the 'Charismatic' banner (in my view) had a natural explanation. I was waiting for an 'Isaac'. 'Isaac' was coming, and when 'Isaac' came, it would be a hundred times greater than anything we had ever seen: proportionately, it would be as much greater than the Charismatic Movement, as Isaac himself, and his promise, was greater than Ishmael.

I made that prophetic statement in 1992, and it got me into an awful lot of trouble, both with charismatics and conservative evangelicals. I simply related to Rodney what I had said two years before, at the same conference centre, without mentioning that the phrase 'Baby Isaac' had come into my mind. But I told him that I had a strong feeling that his ministry was the authentic beginning of what I had prophesied two years before.

That was just a part of what happened that morning. I asked Rodney what he had planned for Saturday morning. He replied that he had nothing planned, and asked what I had in mind. I told him that we as a church are out on the streets every Saturday, and that I would be at the Chapel. I said that I would be very grateful if he would come to the Chapel and just stand in my pulpit and pray. That's all. There wouldn't be anybody there – I would like him to just stand in the pulpit and pray.

Colin Dye spoke up: 'Why don't you do that? You could take your family to see the Changing of the Guard at Buckingham Palace and you'd be right nearby.'

Rodney said he would be glad to come. But then I added one more thing: 'Would you pray for my wife Louise?'

In the previous two or three years, Louise had developed two very serious conditions. I do not know which was worse, or which started first. Probably, one had caused the other. She had a horrible cough. After having had it for two years, her GP sent her to the Royal Brompton Hospital to get it checked out, but they could not help her. We kept thinking that if she went to Florida where the air was clearer she would get better, but she coughed in Florida. The cough was so bad that most mornings I woke up to find that Louise had been up half the night coughing. On most nights she would just get up and sit, rather than wake me up. On the tube, people would move away from her thinking it was contagious: it was embarrassing for her. I've never seen or heard anything like it, and the cough was really getting Louise down. The other condition was a very serious depression from which Louise had suffered for two or three years as well. Whether the cough caused the depression or the depression caused the cough I did not know; all I knew was that it was pretty awful, and I began to wonder how long we could stay in London.

The following Saturday morning, Rodney came to the vestry. He got there before I did and my secretary gave him and his wife Adonica a cup of tea while they waited for us.

'You didn't think I'd come, did you?' said Rodney.

'Well, I wasn't sure,' I replied.

That morning, unbeknown to Rodney, Louise had left a note for me on the kitchen table saying, 'It is 4.30 a.m. and I have just taken a sleeping pill.' My heart had sunk. I thought, 'She's going to miss being prayed for.' But at 9.30 a.m. she got up and said, 'I want that man to pray for me.' She'd only slept for about four hours, but she said, 'I want to go and be prayed for.' This was why we were late, arriving about a quarter to eleven.

I took Rodney into the pulpit at Westminster Chapel and he prayed. As a matter of fact, he read a prayer: it was a prayer that came out of the Welsh Revival. It took him about five minutes to read it. I was surprised that he read a prayer – but that is what he felt led to do and that was fine with me.

Afterwards, we went back to the vestry and I said, 'Now I want you to pray for my wife Louise.' I then told him the afore-mentioned story about what had happened earlier that morning. Rodney asked everybody to leave the room except Louise and I, and his wife Adonica, so his assistant and baby-sitter took his three children out.

Rodney and Adonica began to pray for Louise, while I sat at my desk and watched. Rodney put his hand on Louise's head and shoulder, Adonica put her hand on the other shoulder and Louise's chest and they began to pray. They prayed in tongues. I don't think anything like that had ever happened in the Westminster Chapel vestry before. They prayed for about five minutes. When they had finished, Louise took a deep breath – without any cough! 'I haven't been able to do that in years,' she said, as she took another deep breath, then another. 'I can't believe I didn't cough. I haven't been able to breathe that deeply without a cough for I don't know how long!'

I knew something had happened. After Rodney and Adonica had left, I kept asking Louise, 'Have you coughed yet?' I called her on the phone an hour later: 'Have you coughed?' She replied, 'No!' I called her again an hour after that: 'Have you coughed?' Again, she replied, 'No.' I kept doing it every hour. That night Louise slept like a baby. The next morning I repeated the question, 'Have you coughed?' 'No,' was her reply. She had been instantly healed.

All of this took place in early December 1994. Rodney also invited Louise to attend one of his meetings in America. I knew that she should go. She went to a camp meeting he was holding in Lakeland, Florida. This was January of 1995. While Rodney was preaching, Louise was greatly blessed. She called me after two days and said, 'It is the greatest thing that has ever happened to me. I think it must be the nearest you get to Heaven without dying.' She came back transformed. This time, not only was there no cough – there was no depression either.

But there is more. Our son T.R. was then living in the Florida Keys. Louise called me while she was in Lakeland and asked if I would pray that T.R. would come early to pick her up one day, because she wanted him in the meeting. He came to get her to take her back to the Keys, but was not keen to come early. When he walked into the church and saw strange manifestations he wanted to get out straight away, but he promised to stay, just until 9 o'clock. By eleven o'clock, T.R. was on his feet with his hands in the air, and he never looked back. He was touched by Rodney's ministry and moved back to London.

Soon after T.R. returned to London, he began to watch Rodney Howard-Browne videotapes. He invited a group of young people into his flat and they watched tapes together throughout the summer of 1995. In October 1995, Rodney was preaching in London again, this time for Gerald Coates. About fifteen of our people, mostly those who had been coming to T.R.'s flat to watch Rodney Howard-Browne videos, went to hear Rodney. Louise and I went over later on the Sunday evening and found some of our kids on the floor, having been prayed for by Rodney.

The following Sunday night at Westminster Chapel, I invited all who had been to Rodney's meeting to come to the platform and give a testimony. When they finished, I turned to the congregation and said, 'How many of you would like to be prayed for by these people as well as our deacons, if the opportunity were given?' Nearly every hand went up! That was the night the prayer ministry began at Westminster Chapel. That first night the praying was in the church lounge, and two or three hundred people tried to squeeze into that lounge. A few were on the floor, but not a lot. There were some manifestations, but not many. But a prayer ministry unlike anything that had happened in my experience before had now begun, and we have never looked back.

A year later, John Arnott came to Westminster Chapel and preached for us. We have pews that are fixed to the floor, and so you can't move them out of the way, as you can in many places where they have folding chairs. But this was no problem for John: he prayed for people as they stood, in every other row (those who stayed for prayer) and great blessing followed. He preached twice that day, and the people fell in love with him. His Canadian manner and gentle demeanour endeared him to the people of Westminster Chapel, and it did a lot to help convince people of the authenticity of what was going on. His two sermons were marvellous, and people saw how biblical his preaching was.

In December 1995, one year after having met Rodney Howard-Browne, he preached for us on a Sunday evening in Westminster Chapel. It was a sermon on the Holy Spirit, and I would urge anybody to get a copy of it. Nobody would refute Rodney's orthodoxy if they heard this sermon: it was brilliant. After he preached, he invited people to come forward for prayer. I saw people who had been opposed to this sort of thing transformed that night. One eighty-year-old man was offended when his wife wanted to go up for prayer. She said, 'I want to have Rodney pray for me.'

He said to her, 'Are you really going?'

She replied, 'Yes, I want to go.'

'Well if you go, then I'll go,' he told her.

Rodney prayed for him, and as Rodney prayed the man exclaimed, 'I see Him! I see Him! It's Jesus! It's Jesus!' That man is now in Heaven, having died in 1997, but here was a man who had been utterly biased and prejudiced against this sort of thing at first, but whose life was never to be the same again.

A few moments later, I saw a merchant banker from America, who had been a member of the Chapel, on the floor, rolling back and forth on his back, laughing his head off. He was a very quiet, docile man – not the sort of person you would expect to do that sort of thing. One person after another was blessed. I had never seen anything like it in my life.

I cannot say that Revival has come to Westminster Chapel. There maybe some who would want to say that this is what happened, but, given my definition of Revival, I would say this was not what we are waiting for. And yet I do think God has touched the Chapel. Our prayer ministry still continues. It is not very demonstrative. We have the anointing of oil administered by the deacons, according to James chapter 5 and we have a special area where people come for that if they want physical healing. Others sit anywhere they want in the church and our prayer ministry team goes and prays for them. We have had a number of miracles, but I don't talk a lot about it because we made a covenant with God several years ago that, if He blessed us with signs and wonders, we would not call attention to the signs and wonders, but do what they did in the early church and use the platform to preach the Gospel. This is what we are doing.

DAVID MARKEE

Dave *is married to Ze, and leads Folly's End, a 'Partners in Harvest' church in Croydon, Surrey. Dave is a professional bassist, and has recorded with many famous names including Eric Clapton, Bing Crosby and Joan Armatrading. In 1999 he founded the 'King David Kompany' (KDK), a programme to encourage the restoration of the creative arts within the church. The KDK runs the 'Armed & Dangerous' conferences, bringing together worship, prophecy and intercession.*

DAVID MARKEE

Chapter One

The phone rang – it was my old friend Dan Cutrona, a producer I had known for some time. I had worked with Dan on many projects, playing bass for him in various recording studios. 'Hi Dan,' I said, 'what's up?' (Hoping it would be another bass playing job)

'Got some sessions for you over here later in the year, but this time I'm ringing you in your capacity as a pastor. There's something unusual going on in a Vineyard church here in Toronto. It all seems a bit wacky, but people are saying the Holy Spirit has visited this church in great power and I need a second opinion from someone who I trust. I can't be sure if it's God or not, but you probably need to get over here and take a look.'

Dan knew how passionate we were about the things of God. Almost fifteen years ago, my wife Ze and I had planted a church in south London, while we were still in the music business. Since then it had flourished and gained a reputation for being strongly spirit-filled: God had blessed us with a great church. I was intrigued by Dan's excitement and promised to come out and visit as soon as I could.

Over the course of the next few weeks, I found myself thinking about our conversation a lot, until, one morning Dan called to say that the sessions had been brought forward and were due to start the following week – could I make it? 'Perfect!' I thought. I could go and see what was happening for myself much sooner than expected.

I arrived in Toronto and, at the first opportunity, went to visit what was then known as the Toronto Airport Vineyard Fellowship. As I approached the row of grey, unimpressive buildings, situated virtually at the end of one of the airport runways, I found myself wondering what all the fuss was about. I didn't know what to expect.

My first surprise came when I saw the queue of people waiting to get in stretching down the side of the building. I had only ever seen something like that in a very large church in South Africa, during an International Conference, and yet here were people waiting to get into this little church at lunchtime, and they weren't even holding a conference! 'Something's up,' I thought. As I got nearer the door, I could see that the place was absolutely stuffed with people. My first impression was that there was a great excitement and a real 'buzz' in the air.

The first thing that really impressed me, though, was the worship leader. As he started to sing a song, which I'd never heard before, the presence of God seemed to increase, and I was riveted by the man's tremendous authority in the Spirit: his worship felt so clean. Jeremy Sinnott later became a close friend of mine, as I visited many times over the ensuing years, and I have enjoyed times of worship that he has led many times since, but none more than this first time. I felt welcomed into the Father's presence by Jeremy's sensitivity and grace. He has an unusually powerful 'gathering' anointing, as a father, a pastor, and a great encourager to many. As a true servant of the Lord, he was undoubtedly used powerfully by God, as a major catalyst for the renewal in Toronto and worldwide. The best thing about Jeremy is that he probably doesn't realise just how important his music was to us, and how his presence brought stability to the ministry of Toronto Airport Fellowship, as they sought to steward the fiery outpouring.

'OK, so far so good,' I thought 'What next?' The 'what next' turned out to be what would become a 'signature' of Toronto:

'testimony time'. People were invited onto the stage and asked to describe their recent experience of the Holy Spirit and what had happened to them as a result of the current outpouring. I recognised a fellow Brit on stage: a journalist who was being interviewed by a large man who turned out to be John Arnott, pastor of TACF.

John and his wife Carol seemed to be surprised and delighted that many British people had visited their church already and the numbers were increasing every week. At first, the Brits were mostly from the more traditional renewed wing of the British churches – people from Holy Trinity, Brompton and St Andrew's, Chorleywood – folk who had been affected by the ministry of John Wimber, and had received a good report about the 'blessing'. They had started to come over in increasing numbers. The British press dubbed the phenomenon the 'Toronto Blessing', which opened the doors to even more people from Britain travelling to Toronto from every stream and tribe.

I always enjoyed the testimonies: they brought freshness to the proceedings, as people told of encounters with the fatherhood of God and a renewed sense of His love for them personally. Some would testify to a great filling of the Holy Spirit, some physical healing, and others of emotional healing: but all of them testified to a renewed love for Jesus. 'Why would the devil want to do that?' was one of Pastor John Arnott's favourite questions to any timid believers in the congregation. Each person who gave a testimony was prayed for by a ministry team, who came forward to bless each one. All of them fell down, and most of them were so affected by the prayers that they shook, laughed, cried and manifested some quite bizarre things that I had never seen in church before. I noticed that one of the ministry team had a strange 'affliction', which looked like a nervous motor problem: more than just a 'tic'. He could not go more than thirty seconds without a violent jerking of his head. 'Poor thing,' I thought, 'perhaps he'll get healed if the others pray for him enough.'

Then it was time for the address. As John Arnott took his place at the front of the stage, I was reminded of John Wimber.

Not so much physically, but in the gentle, firm authority and measured tones with which Arnott spoke, which were reminiscent of the laconic style so preferred and pioneered by the Vineyard movement – anti-hype personified! Had it not been for the focus given to the testimony time and the accompanying noises and interruptions, this could have been a classic Vineyard meeting. However, as John spoke, he told us how proud he was of his church members who had to learn to be hosts for the many visitors who were invading them. Revival places a great burden on a local church, and many regular members of TACF had to give up their own seats for the visitors – which they did graciously. Arnott said it was like having twenty extra people show up to every family meal!

John spoke in a wonderfully reassuring way about the Father's love and how small the Devil's power was, in comparison to God's. He quoted one of Wimber's own favourite phrases: 'We must have more faith in God's ability to lead us into truth than the Devil's ability to lead us into error.' However, every time he mentioned how big God was, a man shouted out 'BIG GOD!' at the top of his voice, and interrupted John's flow. There were also many outbreaks of laughter as John spoke. Actually, there were so many noises and interruptions that I couldn't help admiring John's poise as he continued to encourage the congregation to partake of the blessing on offer.

After a while, John announced that it was now 'ministry time' and gave the instruction to 'stack the chairs', which was greeted with excitement as the people moved handbags, coats and belongings out of the way and enthusiastically moved the furniture to clear a space for ministry. He then asked the ministry team to step forward, and asked for volunteers to act as 'catchers', as he did not want anyone to hurt themselves, should they fall down under the power of the Holy Spirit (which most of them did). With the ministry team in place, and the people encouraged to concentrate on Jesus, he then invited the Holy Spirit to come and bless the people. I had seen the Holy Spirit at work many times and in many ways, but I was not prepared for the power with which the Spirit manifested Himself at this meeting. Within two or three minutes, the whole place was transformed from a packed church meeting into something more reminiscent of a battlefield, with bodies strewn about the floor: accompanied by much noise. People were crying out to God with laughter, as well as weeping. Some were making extremely strange noises, and others behaving as though they had just emerged from a heavy session at the pub. Not at all your 'normal' church meeting!

Standing at the back, observing all this, I remembered that on the plane journey to Toronto I had been looking back over the past fifteen years in pioneering our ministry. There were some things that I had never been able to clarify with God to my satisfaction. I wanted to ask Him about them, and had prepared a mental 'shopping list' of questions, ready for any unusual opportunity to hear from God more clearly. I had come expecting to hear from Him and, as I stood watching, I did hear Him speak to me. He asked me a question:

'David, do you think this is me?'

I had to answer with all honesty, 'Yes Lord, I believe this is You, I know You're here and I recognise Your Spirit', even though I was questioning some of the behaviour I saw. His next question nailed me though.

'Well, what are you going to do about it then?'

I find that God often speaks to me in the form of questions, which end up challenging me to respond in some way, so I decided to ditch my shopping list of questions and respond by asking for prayer.

I did this by standing in line with many others and, as I was being prayed for, I heard the pastor's voice saying, 'Lord, send the fire.' I went down under the power of the Holy Spirit and remember thinking, 'How does God want me to receive this fire?' As I lay there, vivid impressions came to me. I sensed a place in my spirit that was pretty fiery, but generally, it seemed as though I was lying in a place like an abattoir, near a gully that led to a drain hole. I gained the impression that something like poison needed to be drained out of me. It was a little confusing at the time, because I was looking for fire. Weeks later, I realised that this was, in fact, exactly what God needed to do in me. He was telling me that there was a deep wound in my spirit that had become infected, and that He wanted to heal it. If you have a deep wound in your spirit, it can burn like fire.

It was announced that there would be a concert on the coming Saturday night at another venue across town. I heard that Brian Doerkson was the artist, and that John Wimber would be there. I love concerts, so I decided to go. I got more than I bargained for.

It was a beautiful early evening and there was a wonderful atmosphere, as young men and women eagerly waited to get into the hall, laughing and joking and generally having a great time. I noticed a young man and woman praying for people in the line, and so I plucked up the courage to go over to ask if they would pray for me when they had finished. About five minutes later, I felt a hand on my shoulder, which signalled the beginning of one of the most wonderful experiences of the Lord I've ever had. As this young man and woman (who I later discovered did not even know each other at the time) laid hands on me and started to pray, the line started to move. After two or three minutes, I was finding it difficult to remain standing and so I leant on the person in front of me. As we got nearer the entrance, I started to feel as if I'd had rather a lot to drink and eventually had to be assisted – almost carried – to my seat in the concert hall. By the time the band was two numbers into the concert, I was absolutely drunk in the Spirit! For the next two hours, these two kept praying for me with stunningly accurate words of knowledge. I believe I was deeply set free and brought much closer to the Father. I was so 'drunk', I cannot remember getting back to the hotel where I was staying, but something significant had taken place in my heart and spirit. I felt like an operation had been performed on my heart. As John Arnott was fond of saying, 'stuff went and stuff came'. (John was great at explaining very deep experiences with very simple language like that, so that the experiences seemed very normal.) Thanks to the Spirit-led prayers of Hilary Dalton and her friend, who had given themselves to pray for someone they'd never met for almost three hours, I was much freer than I'd ever been by the time that concert was over.

Before returning home, I was to visit the church again. This time determined to receive as much as possible from the ministry time. The meeting went well, and when it came time for prayer, I wanted to have the right person pray for me, so I asked the Lord to show me who it should be. My eyes rested on the man with the strange jerking affliction I had seen earlier, and I thought, 'Poor man, he's probably safe enough to get prayer from, after all he'll not be too hard to approach, with a problem like that.'

'Would you pray for me?' I asked him.

'Sure,' he said with a jerk, 'sit down here with me.'

At that moment, a terrible thought entered my head. Were his jerks a manifestation of the Spirit and not a medical problem? If so, it could be catching! 'Lord, whatever You do, please don't give me those jerks – that's the last thing I need to take home with me.'

The aircraft was packed on the journey home. My seat was between two very respectable businessmen. I reckon both of them must have felt sorry for me in my affliction, as I jerked and grunted all the way home. I can't remember spilling anything, or scattering food on them or anyone else, but it's highly possible that I did, as the jerks were strong and totally involuntary.

My wife met me at Heathrow Airport. As I jerked my way through customs, I wondered if my wife, Ze, would think I had contacted some malady overseas. She was waiting for me at the barrier, together with my youngest daughter, Jessica, and as I hugged them both in turn, I tried to control myself. We jerked our merry way out to the car park, with Jessica chattering away, hardly noticing Dad's affliction, and Ze looking at me with a very worried expression, which suddenly seemed like the funniest thing I had ever seen on a human being. By the time I got to the car, I could not speak because I was trying to control not only the jerks, but also paroxysms of laughter. My wife said nothing during the journey home, but Jessica wanted to know everything that had happened. When I told her the stories, she asked me to pray for her. When I did, she said 'Daddy, it feels all fizzy'. I knew what she meant – I had been 'fizzing' in one way or another for the past week or so. They tell me that new wine is unstable and very fizzy too!

As soon as I arrived home, I was on the phone to some of my friends in leadership at the church, and within an hour or so, they started to arrive at our house. I planned to tell them all that had happened to me and then ask if they wanted prayer. For some reason, I felt strongly that I should meet them in our garden. Well, it was a Saturday and a very nice day after all. It seemed a little bizarre, but within a short space of time, I was to see the wisdom in it.

Ze greeted everyone with lemonade and squash and then we all congregated in the garden: those without seats sitting on the grass. The sun shone down as I related my story. I explained about my initial scepticism and my 'shopping list', my surprise at the lack of hype, and the graciousness with which the people of TACF handled the invasion of visitors. They were fascinated as I told how I'd been ministered to for hours and the way I'd been prayed for, and how I'd seen strange things and the Holy Spirit moving in greater power than I'd yet encountered anywhere. Everyone listened very carefully. I asked if anyone wanted me to pray for them, and to my surprise, everyone did! I laid hands on them and invited the Holy Spirit to come.

I had been worried, on the journey home, that despite encouragement to the contrary, the blessing might not be as portable as the TACF leaders said it was. 'What if the Holy Spirit doesn't come?' I thought. I needn't have worried at all, because every single person soon left their upright position as I lightly laid hands on them. The lawn was strewn with recumbent bodies within minutes. The phenomenon repeated itself in church the following Sunday, when I shared my experiences and asked if anyone wanted prayer. They all did, and all 150 ended up on the floor under the power of God. That night we started the first of our evening renewal meetings, which have continued to this day.

I noticed that the Holy Spirit seemed to be going after control issues in people's lives. I quickly came to realise that this is one of the most important things God wants to deal with in the church, in order to get us cleaned up. Many leaders struggle with the issue of control. We need to ask ourselves frequently, 'Who is in charge here – God or me?' I don't know of any pastor who has actually gone into the ministry because of a desire to control people. Leaders know they are called to love and care for people, but sometimes, along the way, we can get entangled in 'running the ministry' and actually end up hurting folk rather than releasing them, as building a better pen becomes more important than taking care of the sheep.

The Holy Spirit showed this to me in a dramatic, but most enjoyable way, when I went into the office the next Monday. My office manager, John Coburn, was at his desk and the two girls were working away. I have always disliked small, fiddly details, and John was a financial bookkeeper who delighted in writing everything down. He came to me with a little plastic packet containing coins amounting to £1.21 and wanted me to sign a receipt. I had just been in the presence of God for an incredible week. I had been on a mountain top with the God who owns the Universe, and here was my financial manager standing there, saying, 'just sign this.' I looked at him, and all sorts of things were going around in my mind. I was thinking, 'How am I going to get this blessing that I've just experienced into the city? How is God going to come in great power, breaking out into revival? How many people are going to be saved and filled with the Holy Spirit? How many marriages are going to be put back together?' – and my financial manager wants me to sign a receipt for £1.21!

I felt anger rise up inside me, and I was just about to open my mouth to challenge him – I wanted to be sarcastic to him. I wanted to ask him, 'How many people is this going to save?' But before I could get anything out of my mouth, I felt the Holy Spirit push me in the back. I literally felt a hand in my back push me and, very slowly, I started to fall over. I fell over my chair and I ended up with my head in the waste paper basket! At that moment, John looked like a very small animal does when it is caught in car headlights! Somehow, I ended up lying under my desk listening to a funny 'knocking' sound. 'What's that?' I thought, and as I looked, I saw that the Holy Spirit had hold of John, and he was bouncing up and down, straight as a ramrod. I started laughing; he started laughing; then the two girls in the office started laughing as well. We all laughed hysterically for about twenty minutes.

I then needed to get up and go to the bathroom, which was through the door and across the corridor. I managed to make it to the bathroom and by this time, both girls were on the floor and John, who was still shaking, had flipped over on his back and was lying under his desk amongst a maze of wires and computer bits, still laughing. As I was coming out of the bathroom, the Holy Spirit hit me again and I ended up, lying flat on my back in the hallway, with one arm in the office door and my leg up the staircase, still laughing.

At that moment, one of my leaders came through the front door. This man had come from a very formal church background and, as he stepped through the door, he found the pastor absolutely 'out of it.' He had brought the Sunday offering and he had to step over me to get into the office, only to find even more chaos. The two girls were wrapped around each other some- where in the corner of the office, and my office manager was flapping like a fish on the floor. The leader told me later that he was very offended by it: but I was not in control of that situation – God was! This leader had a hard time relating to what was hap- pening, because he also had control issues in his own life that God desired to deal with. I thank God that the Holy Spirit gave us laughter while He was working on us: it enabled Him to stuff the truth down our throats while we were still laughing!

Chapter Two

Some of the things we had to deal with in those first few months were awesome. We saw deep, deep issues of pain and sin, and things that we thought were 'under the blood', come roaring up to the surface, as the Holy Spirit exposed dark places that we had, somehow, managed to live with for years. The Lord wanted to teach us how to walk in constant repentance, taking our momentary thoughts captive to Christ and dealing with issues obviously not yet dead enough for Him. We studied much of John and Paula Sandford's teaching, prayed and prayed for each other, and just lay on the carpet for hours. We even invented the 'soaking meeting' where we could come together with no other agenda than to lie on the floor and receive more of the out-pouring of God's Spirit.

As a result, many of us are now in a new place with God. We are more healed and hopefully much nicer to work with, more forgiving, and definitely more in love with Jesus. We've seen whole families healed; marriages put back together; and children, especially, experiencing the power of the Spirit as never before.

Over the last seven years, our church has grown in stature, anointing and maturity and there have been many significant milestones in the church's development. Even though we have not had a 'church planting' policy, churches have been conceived from the womb of Renewal – especially from our yearly *Catch*

101

the Fire conferences held here in Croydon – as newly encouraged and empowered leaders have been challenged to step out
into their destiny.

This book is about the lasting fruit that Jesus desires to culti-
vate in all of us, and to that end I hope and pray that people,
especially Toronto sceptics, will read for themselves what happened to us and what a beautiful blessing we received. Readers
may need to be assured that we are not 'flaky' or weird
Christians, but responsible adults who take their pastoral duties
very seriously. Doubtless, there will be many testimonies in this
book of the incredible healings that have taken place. I too have
received much spiritual and emotional healing from the
'Blessing', as have many people on our leadership team and
throughout our congregation. We are talking about real people's
lives, changed for the better by the power of God. I know these
people and they are not 'flaky'! However, because I am a pastor,
I would like to encourage readers, other pastors and leaders that
our encounter with the blessing also had a very practical effect
on our ministry, and so, I will leave these testimonies for others
to tell and, instead, focus on the incredible acceleration of God's
plan for Folly's End Church, and the growth of the ministry that
we experienced after making the connection with the outpouring
in Toronto.

We had been meeting in a school hall for several years. I knew
that, if we were ever going to make an impact on our city, we
needed a home. One summer, we commissioned a member of our
team to be a 'scout', to go and seek out an appropriate building
in the city. He returned with a report of a derelict building in the
centre of town that had once been a supermarket. It had been
empty for fifteen years and looked like an ideal place for a
church fellowship.

Some years before, my wife, Ze, had received a strong word in
a prayer meeting that we were to 'go to the market-place', and
when I went to see the building, it was in the middle of a 700-
year-old 'fruit and vegetable' market! Long since discarded as a
useful place, it was overrun with pigeons and it stank. I had no

great desire to move the church there, but had a strange feeling that God was calling us to do just that. Reluctantly, I decided to put this to the test. After prayer, I explained to the church that we had seen the building, and said that we would take up a special offering in six weeks' time to test the climate and gauge interest. I then promptly forgot about the whole thing. About 120 adults were present on the morning of the offering. After the meeting, when we counted the offering, the total was a whopping £125,000! I had to sit down at that point: I believe that God had spoken.

Back in 1986, my wife Ze had received yet another very strong word – this time regarding the need for Christian Education. Although neither of us considered ourselves to be educators, nor even very well educated by western worldly standards, we stepped out in faith and began a Christian Primary school. It was pioneered by our middle daughter, Alison and had just nine children in that first year.

God then started to talk to us about a new home for the school, which was also meeting in rented accommodation. I wondered how we could possibly acquire both a permanent church home and a school building at the same time. It seemed like a massive undertaking for a church of 150 people. But as we talked and prayed about it, and believed that, even though we had no money to buy a school building, we should go for it.

There was a lovely old Victorian house not far from where we live and I decided to see if it was available. Unfortunately, it was already under offer to someone else. We needed new accommodation by September and we were already nearing the end of May: we didn't have much time. Still, we felt it was the place that God would provide for the school, so we continued to pray and, within six weeks, the original purchasers had pulled out, our finance was in place, and we had obtained outline planning permission for change of use. Another miracle! Many people helped us with the decorations and we opened Folly's End Christian School with a great celebration just in time for the term to begin. It occurred to me later that God had really put the children first in our plans. It was, only after we had started to get moving with our school that the church home really came together. The pattern was to be repeated some time later with our church School of Ministry and our senior school.

Meanwhile, the original estimate for refurbishing our intended church home had doubled and doubled again, eventually reaching a total of £440,000. But the giving was miraculous: I still don't know today where all of the money came from. I even had a phone call late one night from an old friend who said, 'You're buying a building and I would like to give you some money, but please don't tell anybody who gave it to you'

'Fine by me,' I said, 'how much?'

'£50,000', came the reply. I actually fell on the floor laughing!

Over that time period there were many other wonderful instances of God's great provision, and by the time I stood on the platform of our new church building on the first morning, we only had £60,000 remaining to be paid. I didn't tell the people the figure, because they had been so generous, but when we took the offering that morning, it amounted to £60,045! The people were overjoyed: many people were weeping or laughing. I didn't know what to do, but I couldn't resist asking: 'Lord, what is the £45 for?' I was soon to find out. The following Thursday the young people came into the building and set the fire alarm off. The call out charge was £45! What an awesome God!

I remember being very nervous about our church's new role just before moving into the building and having a conversation with the Lord: 'What on earth am I going to do down there in the market place?'

As usual, He answered my question with one of His own: 'What is in your hand?'

'Worship and music, Lord.'

'Then go to the market place and worship Me.'

Taking Praise to the Gates of the City became a slogan for us, and also became the title of our very first conference in October 1996. Jeremy and Connie Sinnott came over from Toronto, and we had a great time.

Moving into a permanent home with a new auditorium inevitably meant that the whole ministry had to change. Instead of running a 'portable' church where everything was brought in Sunday by Sunday, we had to set up permanent offices and think about how we were to interact with the public day by day. We needed to become a lot more organised. Ze and I spent the next three years locked into administration; daily having to come up with answers regarding how we wanted things to run. Now that was a real stretch! But our meetings, which were continually visited by the Holy Spirit, were strengthening us.

A few years ago, we decided to start our own *Catch the Fire* meetings. John and Carol Arnott came over to Croydon each year for three years. These conferences helped us to establish a city-wide presence and now people come to us from far and wide. Everyone who comes has an encounter with God. It is awesome to see churches and ministries birthed, and many set free. We are so grateful to God for His 'blessing'.

In 1998, we discovered that our building is only 40 metres away from where a great revival took place, under the Jeffreys Brothers. As we stood together and re-opened the Jeffreys' 'well of blessing' with John and Carol that year, I believe we altered something in the spiritual realm. The Jeffreys' movement was largely a healing movement and, recently we have begun holding monthly healing meetings with Ian Andrews.

In 1999, Tommy Tenney visited: which had a huge impact on us. The years beyond 2001 are going to be very exciting, as we plan to take higher ground in our town and see even bigger things.

Almost in a parallel with the way our new building and the junior school came together, was the formation of our School of Ministry [SoM], and the senior section of Folly's End Christian School. Ze and I had been praying about the SoM for two years, but it wasn't until we had decided to go for the senior section of the school that we found the home building for the SoM. God will have us put the children first! Actually they have been sharing the same building and have been a great blessing to one another, and we have been so blessed by them also. What a joy to see upwards of thirty young people becoming like straight arrows, fired out and released into ministry each year. To use a popular catch phrase, we are still very much 'in the river', and this river is taking us forward.

In the heady early days of the blessing, there was much excitement and a wonderful 'buzz' here in the British Isles, as many Britons travelled to Toronto to receive and then bring it all back home. Unfortunately, the enthusiasm seems to have died down a little at the present time in the UK. Although there were reports of great numbers of British churches coming into the blessing, especially during the first two years, many, sadly, now seem to have adopted a 'that was that, now what's next?' attitude. Ministries that were 'going for it' and welcomed the blessing with open arms, have now pulled back, perhaps afraid of the excesses that some experienced. Of course, we all agree that it is absolutely vital to have a balanced attitude towards all things, especially when one is trying to hear God for the direction of a ministry, not to mention one's own family. It all depends on what your idea of balance is. My favourite definition of the word balance is, 'the ability to embrace all valid extremes'. Unfortunately, many view the Lord's will as a very restrictive thing. At Folly's End we have benefited greatly from all the influences that have come our way in our ministry over the years, covering the spectrum from the traditional evangelical wing to the full-on charismatics. All have enriched our lives greatly and given us the opportunity to see our multi-faceted Lord Jesus at work in diverse ways.

While pondering all this, I wondered how an initiative from the Lord that transformed lives and brought such great blessing could be so quickly abandoned. I was troubled by it, and thought about it for some time. Eventually I was reminded of the passage in Matthew 11:3–19 where John the Baptist, in big trouble with the authorities, sends his disciples to Jesus to ask Him a vital question: 'Are You the Coming One, or do we look for another?'[1]

This event provides an amazing insight into our humanity,

seen through the life of John the Baptist, and perhaps contributes towards answering what is a complex question. In times of great spiritual activity, when the Spirit of God comes in power, men and women are initially drawn towards the flame of His presence and taken up by the events, with amazing results, as was John, who had been intimately connected with his cousin, Jesus from his childhood. John knew, without a shadow of a doubt, who the Messiah was, even recognising the Spirit of Jesus from his mother's womb. In later life, he became 'John the Baptizer', whose life message was, 'prepare the way of the Lord'.[2] Living in the wilderness, the man, John, had become a fiery radical, preaching a holiness that knew no compromise with sin. At Jesus' baptism, John saw the Spirit of God descending in the form of a dove and actually heard God's own voice from Heaven, affirming Jesus as the Messiah. There was no real reason to doubt the authenticity of Jesus' claims – they had been fully endorsed from the highest source! And yet, this holy man, who had been thrown into jail and had a death sentence hanging over him, was troubled. Knowing he was shortly going to be martyred for his beliefs, John wanted to know from Jesus' own lips whether he had laboured in vain. Under mind-numbing pressure and assailed by doubts, he sent his friends to Jesus to ask, 'Are You the Coming One, or do we look for another?'[1]

Churches and leaderships initially touched by the power of the Holy Spirit in 1994, afterwards experienced pressure from within the Church as well as the press. Church leaders, community leaders and Toronto sceptics launched, what were at times, scathing attacks on those who supported the move of the Spirit. For some, the high cost of 'staying in the river' was, by comparison, a small price to pay for the blessing received. Others were not willing to maintain their position in the face of opposition and got out of the river. Others it seems were not fully convinced and could not help asking the same question as John the Baptist: 'Is this it, or should we look for something else?' and quietly shifted emphasis, allowing the river merely to ebb towards the margins of their ministry. Jesus lovingly answered His cousin John with the words: 'Go and tell John the things you have seen and heard: the blind see, the lame walk, the lepers are cleansed, the deaf hear, the dead are raised, the poor have the gospel preached to them. And blessed is he who is not offended because of Me'.[3]

To those who would question the validity or the lasting effects of the Toronto Blessing, may I humbly submit the testimony of my own eyes: I have seen a mighty move of God, which has blown across the Nations. The lame have walked, the deaf have heard and the poor have had the gospel preached to them. Many people have been healed, delivered and set free, and are now enjoying a fresh and beautiful intimacy with their Saviour. The blessing is still here, active in our church and elsewhere. We do not really need 'something else' or the next thing, we just need more of what we have been given already. We need not take offence, or to be ashamed of this wonderful blessing from the Father. 'Thanks be to God for His indescribable gift!'[4]

NOTES

[1]Matt. 11:3
[2]Is. 40:3
[3]Matt.11:4–6
[4]2 Cor. 9:15

PAUL REID

Paul is the Leader of the Lifelink team, a group of churches in Ireland committed to church planting and resourcing other churches. He is also Senior Pastor of Christian Fellowship Church in Belfast. He travels extensively, and has a vision to see the nations reached in his lifetime. Paul is committed to reconciliation in his own country, and is firmly committed to the principle of the unity of all believers, which he sees as essential if the Church is going to effectively reach the world. He is married to Priscilla, and they have four daughters.

PAUL REID

Chapter One

There I was, standing in my pyjamas in the hotel lobby, surrounded by people I knew and recognised from church. I had a burning candle in my hand and, as I directed its light towards each of their familiar faces, I asked, 'Do you want more of God?' They replied, 'Yes.'

I don't often have dreams that are as significant, but this one was special. It woke me from my early morning sleep that summer's day in 1994. The dream had such an impact on me that I went downstairs and began to rewrite my sermon for later that day. It was entitled, 'Preparing to Receive a Move of God.'

At that point, we had heard a little of what was going on in Toronto. We knew God was doing something, but what specifically, we had little idea. We had even less idea that we would fit into the picture: our minds and hearts were elsewhere. Our church had gone through some turbulent times in the previous year and a half.

To begin with, God had challenged us to turn our Sunday evening celebration into a prayer meeting. We saw numbers plummet from five hundred people to around one hundred. However, we went through with it, because we believed the Lord was warning us that if we didn't start praying, then we wouldn't have a church in a year's time. Six months later, in September 1993, we faced yet another problem. A major leadership crisis

111

had led to a very difficult year: all we could do was cry out to God. Our plea was simply, 'Lord, we need You'.

It was in January 1994 that we first heard of what was happening in Toronto from one of our former church elders. He had emigrated to Canada several years before, and had gone to Toronto Airport Christian Fellowship. One day, he called to tell us about the strange things that had happened in the church the previous weekend, with people falling, crying and laughing during the service. But that was it. We heard nothing more until a few months later, when reports reached us that the Holy Spirit was touching people in a new way. Holy Trinity, Brompton, in London was experiencing a move of God. This time it was on this side of the Atlantic, and we realised that whatever was happening, it was moving closer to us.

Initially, I was resistant when I heard that people were flocking to Canada. At that time, my view was that people shouldn't have to travel any distance in order to experience God. He could be encountered anywhere and at anytime. However, my wife, Priscilla, pointed out that if God were blessing people in the hotel across the road from our church, then I'd probably make the effort to go. My attitude changed.

'Please God, show me what to do. I need some clear direction on this one', I cried to God one Sunday evening. Priscilla had suggested that I should travel to Toronto to see firsthand what was happening. But I was uncertain, and besides I couldn't afford a trip abroad. So I decided to do something I don't usually do: I decided to put out a 'fleece' and ask God for confirmation. The next day, when I awoke, a postcard had arrived from a friend in London. She told me that there was a real move of God in Toronto, and pointedly asked, 'When are you going to get involved?' Later that day I confided in another friend about the possibility of travelling to Canada. Without saying much, he gave me a cheque for £500, and indicated that it might prove useful for the trip. God was obviously trying to tell me something. There and then, I decided I would go.

A week later it was announced in church that I was planning

to visit Toronto. Eleven other people agreed to join me. By this stage, there was an incredible buzz in church, and people wanted to know what was going on. Something was happening that we'd never experienced before. We were dry; we were hungry; and Toronto was the next step for us.

The more he trembled and shook, the more annoyed I became. I put my Bible up to the side of my face to shield him from view, and as I did, I fell to the ground laughing. I laughed and laughed all through that first evening service. We had arrived in Toronto the previous day, and had been invited to join the Airport Christian Fellowship on their summer retreat. A man across the aisle had been distracting me throughout the meeting: I though he was being irreverent. However, within seconds, I was no longer a spectator, but a participant. The Holy Spirit came upon me, and I found myself lying on the floor in fits of laughter. I can recall thinking that if I had been the preacher at the meeting I would have had me thrown out. It wasn't that I was out of control, but I simply couldn't stop laughing. I nipped myself in the arm to sober up, but nothing seemed to work. I thought about my cat dying. But it was no use. The laughter continued for over two hours, and by the end of it, I felt like a complete and utter wreck.

Of course, unknown to me at the time, most of the rest of the team had had a variety of strange experiences. I remember one night seeing three of them lying in a row, laughing their way through the meeting. They would probably all agree, though, that I was affected even more than the rest of the team. During the week I was invited to speak on several occasions, but I was always 'too far gone' to say anything. As soon as the service started I would slump to the ground, and remain there until it was over. There is no doubt that leaders are the gateway to the church, and I think the Lord deliberately did what He did to me, so that I could lead the way. Looking back, it was absolutely bizarre. I'd never experienced anything like this. I wasn't quite sure what was going on, but I felt privileged that God had touched me. However, this wasn't just for me, or for the rest of the team, it was for the whole of our church. And it wasn't long before they too experienced the move of God, which we had encountered in Toronto.

'There's been a massacre,' cried one of the children at the end of our very first meeting back in Belfast, as they encountered bodies strewn across the church floor. We had arrived back from Toronto the day before, and people had flocked to our Sunday celebration, eager to hear what had happened. But there wasn't much to hear. As soon as Robin Mark, our worship leader played a few chords things began to happen. I was the first to fall to the ground; then some people started shaking. Others were agog. We offered to pray for people. The first person to come forward, fell down and howled like a baby. Suddenly, there was an almighty release of something. Whoosh! It swept right across the congregation. It was like a Pentecost experience.

More and more people collapsed. Those left standing didn't know what to do. Priscilla decided to take control of the situation, but as she walked to the front she fell against a wall, and began to prophesy in a way she had never done before. She prophesied about specific countries and nations. As I lay on the floor, amid the shouting and noise, I recall thinking, 'I recognise the sound of that voice'. The place was in total uproar: even young children were falling down. Some people were worried: they had never witnessed anything like this before, and had no yardstick to measure it by. Some said, 'Oh no! We're going to leave this church', while others reacted, 'This is what we've been waiting for.'

That evening, we returned to church for the Sunday prayer meeting. The building was packed full of people who'd heard reports of our morning service. A man sat beside me in the front row. He looked around, before turning to me, and said, 'This is a great crowd for the prayer meeting'. I smiled: 'I take it you weren't there this morning.'

Ironically, one of the most significant things to happen to me in the following weeks took place, not in Belfast, but back across the Atlantic. Months before, a church and Bible college in Portland, Oregon, had invited me to preach at their weekend retreat. When I arrived, the word was out about Toronto. People were discussing what they'd heard through the grapevine. Many of them appeared to be extremely cautious about it all. Little did they know that I had not only been to Toronto Airport Christian Fellowship, but had experienced firsthand this move of God.

Imagine the shock when, at the first meeting, I asked people to close their Bibles, and then shared with them what I had encountered in Toronto. Some of them were horrified that I would do such a thing. After I'd spoken, the seats were moved aside, and I offered to pray for people. As I did so, many of them fell to the ground.

As the weekend came to an end, I encouraged the pastor to go to Toronto, so that he could judge for himself whether or not this really was from God. Gladly, he took up my challenge and made the trip. Two months later, he wrote to me to say that his attitude had changed. The 'Toronto Blessing' was as real for him as it had been for me. The church was later to become a centre for renewal in the north west of the United States.

'Toronto Blessing Claims Another Minister', declared the local newspaper headline. As we began to hold bi-weekly 'soaking meetings' in Belfast, other churches throughout Ireland followed suit. God was working particularly strongly in the Church of Ireland, where several clergymen had organised their own 'refreshing' services in places like Omagh, Monkstown and Dublin. It was small, but significant. However, alongside this desire to experience more of God, came an increase in criticism. A rural Presbyterian church in County Antrim forced its minister out after he tried to introduce 'refreshing' meetings. The Sunday service ended in a fight between some members of the congregation. It captured the imagination of the newspaper headline writers.

The heat of criticism intensified over the following months, as the 'Toronto Blessing' became more widespread. In spring 1995, we organised a major conference with Marc Dupont from Toronto. Each night, around 1,200 people packed into the Presbyterian Church's Assembly Buildings in Belfast. It was a venue that was accessible to many from within the mainstream churches. In the crowd were two newspaper reporters who photographed people lying on the floor. The pictures made the front-page lead in the local Sunday press. Some Christians were outraged. The Presbyterian Church prohibited us from using the building again and only recently did it lift the ban. However, the publicity, which fuelled some people's fears, also raised the interest of many others. By Easter 1995, over 2,500 people were ready to experience more. They travelled from all over Ireland to hear John and Carol Arnott and Marc Dupont speak at our *Together for the Kingdom* conference in Mosney, near Dublin. It was probably the most powerful event we have ever organised, and it helped put the 'Blessing' firmly on the map of Ireland. To this day, people still talk about it, testifying that God did something dynamic in their lives.

'He's no longer the man I married,' exclaimed one woman, as she told me how her husband had been dramatically changed that Easter weekend. God had touched him, and there were many others too. In particular, I received many letters from people sharing about how they had encountered God's love. And that wasn't surprising, given that Northern Ireland is such a legalistic society, where we often find ourselves arguing about His grace. One man wept as he recounted to me how before, he used to wake up everyday praying, 'I need to love You more, God'. But since his experience, he has begun to think, 'I don't realise how much You love me, Lord'. Things have changed. He was always striving to love God more, when what he needed to know was how much God loved him.

Chapter Two

So, what was going on? After our first Sunday meeting in Belfast, I had to gather my thoughts and give an explanation. That Sunday had quite obviously, and somewhat unexpectedly, been a visible demonstration of the power of God: the verbal explanation came the following week. However, that wasn't easy, because it was all so new to me. Nonetheless, I went ahead, and told the congregation that what had happened appeared to be a sovereign outpouring, an impartation from God, which you 'caught' once you were prayed for, and then could 'pass on' to others. Biblically, such things happened at times, like when the Holy Spirit fell in power on people in Acts 2. Looking back, though, I believe I was too quick to try to explain. I did so because I wanted to reassure people that we weren't mad. But I think that if it were to happen again, I'd probably take more time to consider it and think it through.

As the weeks passed by, I recognised a pattern emerging. Firstly, there were people who jumped right in with both feet. Nothing could stop them from receiving God's blessing. Secondly, there were the late adopters. I think some of them initially thought, 'Let's batten down the hatches and endure it. It'll all be over within a year': they held back to begin with, and analysed the situation, before going for it and joining in. And lastly, there were those who came forward, and nothing

117

happened. At the time, we made the mistake of thinking that they found it hard to receive or were not open, and believed that they were missing out on what God was doing. However, we quickly rejected that view. The real issue was not whether someone was shaking or laughing, but what God was doing inside; whether God was changing their life?

I admit that, given the mood of the day, we tended to concentrate on the physical manifestations. But then, on most occasions, they pointed to the fact that something was happening within. In my own case, people couldn't deny that I'd been affected. On some occasions, while I was preaching, I would suddenly burst into tears, and couldn't continue for sobbing. That made an impact on people, especially on those who know how measured I usually am.

Being a black and white sort of person, I was absolutely convinced that this was of God. But there were plenty of critics and cynics too. Several friends rebuked me over what was happening. They were genuinely afraid that God's name would be brought into disrepute. I received nasty letters and anonymous telephone calls from people condemning the whole thing. A handful of people left the church. Some others accused me of not keeping a tight enough rein on things. But what they didn't understand was that I was frightened of offending the Holy Spirit: I was prepared to let almost anything go. Later, we formed a ministry team as a safeguard, restricting the number of people who could offer prayer.

There were others who voiced concern that we were being deceived. Of course, I don't deny that there was a mixture of the flesh, the Devil and the Holy Spirit in it all. But God was in it in a very big way. There were some occasions when, perhaps, things happened that weren't from God. But it was in a much smaller measure than critics give us credit for. Despite all the clamour and knocks from the outside, and mistakes on our part, I believe God was genuinely at work.

'Do we want to be a revival centre, or do we want to build community?' was the question we had to ask ourselves. Was this move of God a 'bless me thing', or was the Lord trying to say something deeper to us? Many months later, we set up seven working groups of ten people each, who were not in key leadership positions, and asked them questions about the church. The survey suggested that people missed the sense of community in church. It was then decision time. We had to choose whether to continue with our refreshing meetings, or concentrate on rebuilding community. We decided on the latter and organised cell groups as a result. They enabled us to recapture something of that desire for togetherness.

The 'Toronto Blessing' led us to organise a series of forty-day prayer and fasting initiatives, and to pray at 6 o'clock every morning for a year. Since then, the church has gone through ebbs and flows. There have been times when nothing much has happened, and then suddenly, things have begun to roll again. Some people would argue that we've moved on from Toronto. However, I would contend that we're continuing with what God began in 1994. That powerful move of the Holy Spirit helped shape us into the church we are today.

Our church is in an area, which has, perhaps, the highest concentration of churches in the whole of Western Europe. Despite that, huge numbers of people no longer have any links with a particular church. Our primary focus is to touch a growing generation that has no spiritual or religious affiliation. What makes us distinct is that we do not have a denominational label. We're committed to the principle that there is one 'new man' in Christ. There has always been a third dissenting voice in Irish religious life. We feel part of that, which means that we're neither Catholic nor Protestant. It's not that we're denying our background, but the reality is that we want to express something different. Every generation has a prophetic message, which translates the gospel into something that's meaningful. In Northern Ireland, it has to touch on the subject of the church being divided, of reconciliation and of peace. If the Gospel hasn't anything to say about that, it really doesn't have anything to say at all.

Another of our priorities is working with marginalised people. East Belfast is a highly deprived area, with large levels of unemployment, and racketeering by loyalist paramilitaries. We have been involved in facilitating projects among the jobless, and single mums. Recently, we purchased a disused pub of 5,000 square feet, which now houses a play-school, restaurant, and training and employment centre. Ten years ago, someone prophesied over me and said that in the future the Government would give us millions of pounds. That seemed bizarre at the time, but in the last twenty-two months, we have received over £600,000 in grants from Government agencies and various funds.

Over the years, the church has grown significantly, and several churches have been planted throughout Northern Ireland and the Republic of Ireland. Looking to the future, we already have plans to expand further, by planting a congregation in rural mid-Ulster, later this year. The whole thing is about flexibility. We are prepared to try new things, and what's more, we're not afraid to admit it when they don't work.

I'm convinced that God doesn't give us a map – He gives us a guide, the Holy Spirit, to direct us along the way. As we have journeyed, there is no doubt that God used the 'Toronto Blessing' to affect our church. Firstly, it made us think about the sort of church we wanted to become, and opened us up to the possibility of change. We are now flexible about how we 'do church' in a post-modern world. We're ready to try new things. Secondly, personal ministry was given a high value. Praying for people in our cell groups and after meetings is part of what we are as a charismatic church. But Toronto helped open up more people to ministry.

I believe Toronto was a catalyst, which broke the spirit of control on churches. It was a time when the Lord was allowed to do what He wanted. God revealed the paradox that while He's always the same, we cannot predict what He's going to do next. He broke out of the theological box that most of us had packed Him into. Solomon once said, 'Behold, heaven and the heaven of heavens cannot contain You. How much less this temple which I have built!' (1 Kings 8:27). Solomon was a wise man. He caught hold of a reality many years ago, which we have only recently come to grasp. God cannot be limited: Toronto certainly confirmed that.

STUART BELL

Stuart *is married to Irene and has three children. He leads New Life Christian Fellowship in Lincoln, and also leads the Ground Level Team, which serves a growing network of churches. His ministry also involves extensive travel, and leading the annual 'Grapevine' event at the Lincolnshire Showground.*

STUART BELL

Chapter One

One morning, early in 1994, I was fascinated by a headline in the daily newspaper. 'It Wasn't My Fault Says Vicar'. The article spoke about strange happenings in a rural Anglican church. As the vicar blessed the congregation some fell to the floor, others laughed, or cried. I instinctively connected these happenings with revivals in church history, and was eager to find out more. In the following weeks I heard reports of how Holy Trinity Church, Brompton, had been impacted by the Holy Spirit after a visit by a lady called Ellie Mumford, who had visited Toronto Airport Christian Fellowship, Canada. After sharing her testimony, other churches in London were also affected, such as Wimbledon Baptist Church and networks of new churches. Secular newspapers were reporting of a 'Toronto Blessing' affecting British churches. I was eager, at this point, to find out more and I rang my good friend, Gerald Coates, who oversees the Pioneer network of churches. He informed me that exciting things were happening in the London area. I was determined that if this was a genuine move of the Holy Spirit, although Lincoln was somewhat off the beaten track, I would do my best to get in the way of this blessing.

In May 1994, Dr R. T. Kendall visited us here in Lincoln to speak at a Leaders conference on the subject 'Word and the Spirit'. His visit turned out to be life changing. In a very humble way, Dr Kendall spoke of how he had changed his opinion concerning the so-called 'Toronto Blessing'. At first, he had warned members of Westminster Chapel not to be involved, but after questioning leaders from Holy Trinity, he began to endorse the move as genuine. At the end of his stay with us in Lincoln, Dr Kendall prayed with a small group of us, asking God that if in any way he was a carrier of this blessing that we would know a fresh anointing of the Holy Spirit. Before leaving he said, 'If anything happens in your ministry during the next twenty-four hours let me know, first class'. Little did I expect the events of the following day!

I drove to a conference centre in Sizewell, Suffolk, where I spoke to around seventy leaders from the Ichthus fellowship. The meeting was one of the most memorable I have ever attended. It seemed to me that God invaded the room, and it is hard to describe the variety of activities that took place: some laughed, some cried, other publicly confessed sins, and it was a humbling and moving day. On my way home, I stopped to speak at a leadership forum in Newark, Nottinghamshire. It was a very low-key evening but, at the end, the leaders asked if I would pray with them. To my amazement, the same phenomena I had seen at Sizewell were also present there.

In the days that followed, I saw great blessing come to my family and to the church. It seemed that the blessing I had received was infectious and made a deep impression on the leadership of our church and members of the Ground Level Team, with whom I am also involved. All were freshly anointed with the Holy Spirit.

During a ministry trip to America, I decided to visit Toronto Airport Christian Fellowship for the first time, with my friend, Jack Groblewski, from Pennsylvania. We had a problem finding the church, which was situated at the end of a runway (this was before the fellowship moved to new prestigious premises). On a cold November evening, we stood in line, along with hundreds of others, waiting for the meeting to begin. Taxis arrived with people from many different nations. Jack and I just made it into the main meeting area: others filled an overflow room to watch the proceedings on closed-circuit television. I was impressed at how ordinary everything was. The worship was led by a group of young musicians. The worship leader, who wore a baseball cap back-to-front, led us in exuberant praise. It was quite some time before I found out who was leading the meeting and, even then, I wasn't sure whether this was a leader of the church or not, as John and Carol Arnott were away on ministry at the time.

Afterwards, Jack and I stood in line waiting for prayer. Those who prayed for us were caring and sensitive and within a few moments, Jack and I were laid side-by-side laughing uncontrollably. This was deep and joyful laughter that, somehow, brought health and life to both of us. In our hotel, later, Jack and I were given 'knowing' looks as we were clearly among the noisiest delegates. We remained for three days of prayer and gave God space to work in our lives. Following this experience, ministry became a delight, and often, just by sharing my testimony, God would move in wonderful ways in people's lives.

One of my most memorable ministry trips was to Pittsburgh, Pennsylvania, where Bill and Melinda Fish, who pastor the Church of the Risen Saviour, welcomed me. During this visit, I became aware of the depth of the work of the Holy Spirit, as I witnessed many people, united, from many backgrounds and denominations, deeply touched by God's presence. These remain holy memories for me. Later, I visited Toronto again, to hear Dr Kendall minister.

My next visit to Toronto was as a guest speaker at their Pastor's Conference. I had previously met John and Carol Arnott at a conference in Brighton, hosted by Terry Virgo. I found them to be very unassuming and honest people, who I sensed have a great compassion for those who are hurting. They spent hours praying for people, and consistently made themselves available to serve. It was at this conference that John invited me to come and speak in Toronto. This was a great honour for me, and a number of people from my church accompanied me. Although the meetings were to be broadcast to thousands, I felt no sense of intimidation, but rather of being affirmed and welcomed as part of their team for the conference. My wife, Irene, and I felt as though we were walking in the favour of God and our lives were deeply affected.

In the summer of 1999, I returned once more to Toronto, to share at the *Take Another Drink* conference, where the emphasis was for people to spend as much time as possible just soaking in the presence of God.

A number from our network of churches have visited Toronto during the last six years, and all have returned with a positive report of what the Lord has done. Most of our churches would testify to the enrichment they received during this time, and many leaders' meetings and celebrations have been of a new order. In Lincoln, we have had the privilege of praying for thousands of people. From 1994–1998, we held 'refreshing meetings' on a weekly basis, and many people travelled from all over the country to be there. At our *Grapevine Celebration*, which takes place every August Bank Holiday weekend, at the Lincolnshire Showground, we have known exciting moves of the Spirit over the last few years. Many testified of a new sense of the presence of God.

As a church, we have no formal links with Toronto Airport Christian Fellowship, but relationally, want to identify with those who are 'in the river' and want to go on record as affirming John and Carol Arnott and their staff who, selflessly, have given away the love of God. Their attitude and service, often under criticism and pressure, have been of the highest order and the church worldwide has been blessed through their servanthood and faithfulness.

Chapter Two

'I will never be the same again, I can never return I've closed the door, I will walk the path I'll run the race, and I will never be the same again.'[1] In 1994, I was profoundly touched by a new sense of anointing, as God's presence seemed to be so close.

I was brought up in a Methodist household and my dad was a local preacher for twenty-five years. During my childhood, I was brought up to love Scripture and to recognise the sense of the presence of God. From around the age of eight, I remember having a strange fascination for revival and a longing to see God move in power. In my late teens, I was introduced to Pentecostals and became aware of a missing dimension in my life. Very soon, I experienced the baptism in the Holy Spirit and enjoyed fruitful years during the charismatic move of the 60's and 70's. For as long as I can remember, I have always had a desire to go beyond religious routines and looked for a passionate faith and, very quickly, I embraced what was flowing through Toronto. I suppose, due to my Methodist roots, I was looking for a movement of God similar to the days of the early Methodists, when the region in which I live was affected greatly by the power of the gospel.

Over the last six years, pastorally, I have had a measure of disappointment. I was saddened by the heavy criticism of some Christians in the early days of 1994 who, in my opinion, had not adequately looked into the issues. In the context of our local church, I felt, from the beginning, that it was important to major on scripture, and also to comment on and read extracts from past revivals. This, I believe, has kept us from any sense of division in the church: for although things were very different we did, I believe, put everything into a scriptural context. A number, who initially embraced the move and then began to back off, also saddened me. This led me into a study of the scriptures, where Solomon, after building the temple, knew a great move of God's presence, as fire came down, and yet his life did not change.[2] I became aware that it was possible to be 'touched, but not changed'. I became aware that every move of the Spirit, in a sense, needs 'stewarding'. In the words of Paul Scanlon, a friend of mine from Abundant Life Church, Bradford, 'We need to manage the miracle'. I believe it was this understanding that helped us here at New Life Christian Fellowship, Lincoln, to see most of the church affected, to some degree. We did our best to give some kind of explanation for the things that were taking place, and when we were uncertain, we were not afraid to say so. Not everyone was fully blessed, but most saw this as a genuine move of God, which has refreshed us and given us a growing vision to reach out into the city and area with the gospel.

The last six years have seen a great acceleration in terms of those involved in mission, and our vision to reach our city has been renewed. In a sense, we were not taken by surprise in 1994 because Dale Gentry, a prophet from USA, had spoken a prophetic word over us in 1991. We have had an increased sense of the holiness of God, which has affected our worship and our mission. Prayer has also taken on a new dimension, with passionate intercessors giving themselves sacrificially to support the team. I have not seen renewal in terms of an addition to church life, but rather it has continued to be the life flow of all the activities that we are involved with. Not everyone would connect their activity with the renewing work of the Spirit, but I would have to say that spiritual activity, in terms of reaching out in mission, care for the poor and the presentation of the gospel, has accelerated greatly throughout this period.

As a leadership team, we have no desire to go back to church as it was, but I am aware that refreshing, in a sense, is not an end in itself, but is for a purpose. The strong dynamic of the Spirit that we encountered in '94 and '95 in particular, is not among us in the same degree, but I genuinely believe there has been a deepening work of God that has touched the very foundation of our lives. We are also aware that, whenever we give room for God, He keeps coming. Our prayer is, 'keep coming, Holy Spirit'. I want to continually be open to 'receiving', but the emphasis increases on the 'giving away' element. There is a world out there to reach. I have learned, however, that pro-grammes and heavy-duty pressure are not going to achieve what we long for.

It seems to me that some churches have seen the 'Toronto Blessing' as an experience to 'go through', and that now, other agendas are more important. I don't see it that way. I do not want to return to the concepts of human effort to produce what we are looking for. To me it was amusing that God visited Britain, after a season of particularly heavy activity. I believe these were God-given initiatives. We saw the 'Jim' campaign, the 'Minus to Plus' initiative and a number of denominational mission enter-prises, all good in themselves, but it was as though after all our hard work God came in a surprising and sovereign way. Again, it reminded me of all the activity in building the Temple as in the days of Solomon. After all the activity, 2 Chronicles 7:1 states, 'When Solomon finished praying, fire came down from heaven and consumed the burnt offering and the sacrifices; and the glory of the Lord filled the temple'. I believe in many ways the church can do less in terms of programmes and meetings and achieve more as we give room for the Holy Spirit's work. As a pastor, I have found this a difficult balance to keep. I believe the refresh-ing of the Holy Spirit has led to activity that is more productive.

NOTES

[1] 'I Will Never Be The Same Again', Geoff Bullock (1996, Word Music).

[2] 1 Kings chapters 6–11; 2 Chronicles chapters 7–9.

PAUL WAKELY

Paul has been an elder of Bath City Church since 1986, serving particularly in the area of pastoring and teaching. A former music teacher, he is married to Sue and they have five children. He and Sue are also involved in a growing network of local churches.

PAUL WAKELY

Chapter One

As I entered the 90's, the gap between what I knew in my head and what I knew in my heart was quite wide. I was operating, more out of principle, than out of genuine convictions and experiences in my own heart. Several deep struggles were coming to a head: battles to believe in myself, coupled with fear of rejection – all while in a leadership position at Bath City Church.

In 1993, a close friend came to give a series of talks to us, in which he described the state of the church in general, by referring to the story of the disciples in their boat on the lake. They were actively engaged in doing something, but without Jesus, and they got into serious difficulties. His basic point was that we too were like this. For four nights, he spoke about the crucial role of the Holy Spirit, and as I listened, I thought, 'I don't know this'. It whetted my appetite for more of God. I felt that in our particular church setting, we were working incredibly hard, but not moving forward significantly. At that time, we did not have the understanding of God's ways that we really needed and, consequently, did not know what we *should* be doing as a church.

Then in 1994, we started to get news that there were signs of an outpouring of the Holy Spirit happening at various places in Britain. My fellow elder, David Dalley, and I, went to Birmingham, and saw Rodney Howard-Browne just praying 'fill, fill, more, more', while people were laughing and so on in the congregation. Meanwhile Clive Jackson, the friend who taught that 'Disciples in the boat' series, went to Toronto, to the airport church. This was the first time I had had any direct contact with it, and he phoned me from there, completely 'drunk' in the Holy Spirit. I didn't feel at all apprehensive about it, but rather, very hungry. We shared with the church our sense that something was going on, and we decided to ask the Holy Spirit to come in that same way in Bath.

We duly went ahead, but found ourselves completely out of our depth in terms of what was happening all around us. All of the Holy Spirit manifestations, which are now familiar, were completely new to us then, and people were literally just crashing around the place, rolling around on the floor: it was complete chaos. Later that day, some friends and I spent time praying, and for two or three hours, we were just laughing and experiencing great joy – totally 'drunk' in the Spirit. (The experience really did remind me of times when I had been drunk in the past, before I was saved, only without the unpleasant aspects.) Now, I felt the closeness of Jesus Himself.

A lot of what went around that summer of '94 was 'out-of-control', yet we had a growing sense that this really was the Lord. Bryn Jones, who led Covenant Ministries, who we were affiliated to at the time, had encouraged many related church leaders to be open to this and, when Dave got back from a ministry trip, he too basically said 'let's go for it'.

The first time I actually made a trip to Toronto was for the *Catch the Fire* conference that took place in October of that year. I went with my wife, Sue, and it was all very new to us. We had seen some dramatic occurrences back home but, in Toronto, we found three times the power and three times the upheaval! There was an immensely powerful sense of God, in a way that was completely new to me: people were sometimes being affected very powerfully, as God moved on them, and they would respond in a strong physical way – yet it all felt very safe. Again, I felt very hungry for what God had to offer. At the meetings I often fell to the floor – sometimes numb, often feeling very moved. I was unsure what to expect but, I felt comfortable with it. I remember that the worship was extremely passionate and abandoned. I was, more than anything, just desperate that God would get to me, calling out: 'Have me, rescue me, revive me Lord! I'm hungry'.

For me, this was the beginning of a new discovery of the Love of God, and I was particularly struck by the way John Arnott showed love to and honoured everyone. I was most impressed with John, who seemed to be a man of real integrity. He had let go of so much, but had retained the right kind of authority, within which, there was immense freedom and huge encouragement to respond to God. He kept repeating a phrase to explain what was happening: that it was 'God coming to love His people back to life', and that really felt right. It was the beginning, in me, of that crucial movement from head to heart.

On that first visit, Sue and I were there for just a few days, but we were eager to return and, in particular, to have a chance to just stay there and 'hang out'. This opportunity was afforded by a non-conference visit in 1997, when we were able to stay for a week and open ourselves up to the kind of healing we both knew we needed inside. It started very low key: I was geared up for lots of ministry but, for a few days, we just watched the video series of John and Paula Sandford, who are known worldwide, for their teaching on inner healing. The goal was that, as issues arose for us, out of the subjects they addressed such as judging others, or making inner vows, failing to forgive, and so on, we would then begin to pray into those areas with the couple from the Toronto team who we were staying with. And they provided a terrific starting point for us.

We felt we were 'ripe' for this. We had been praying a lot for other people and had seen God move, but realised that we needed more of Him ourselves, and there were barriers which needed removing before this could happen. As Sue and I pursued the Sandford teaching, the Holy Spirit began revealing the nature of God as a father, showing us His kindness and His mercy. I kept hearing this, of course, but had realised that there was a lot of pain and rejection in me, making it difficult for me to receive this. The Lord began to expose the roots of my insecurity and, since then, God has continued to heal my heart considerably. The more I've discovered that He really enjoys me and that He is, indeed, a true father, the more deeply I have felt safe and secure. Before I had this revealed to me, rejection held me and gripped me. As a leader, I had been trying to prove myself, trying to 'make it'. Now I feel like a new foundation is being put in, and that process is advancing; continuing to deepen in me.

It was a natural consequence of our experiences that we encouraged members of our church to visit Toronto as well, and we actively still do. I believe that there are places which God 'visits', where He particularly pours out His Spirit. Yes, there is always a danger, in these situations, of just running around, endlessly seeking out the latest thing, but it is the lasting fruit of this move in Toronto that impresses me. For instance, attending the School of Ministry in Toronto profoundly changed my teenage son Johnny. In him, in the people there, in the leadership, I sense a kind of hallmark, which I love. They are clearly changed, so they now possess healed, tender hearts, and a humility, a vulnerability and an ability to impart something which they have truly and deeply received from God. Underlying it all, there is a rest in God, and a dependence on the Holy Spirit, without any sense of striving.

In my opinion, the fact that John Arnott and his people were already being influenced by the Sandford material, with its emphasis on healing the heart, probably made it easier for them to receive from God. It seems to me that John Arnott is a real apostle of love: I never once heard a whisper of pride in all the time I was with him. We continue to be amazed by the way God is healing and restoring His people in Toronto, mobilising a 'healed-up' army. The fruit there seems to have gone deeper, and their passion for harvest – to reach the unsaved – has increased.

Since our initial visits to Toronto, we have had numerous speakers and visitors who are part of the Toronto team, either from the School of Ministry, or the actual leadership, come to

Bath City Church. In 1998, John and Carol Arnott came over and led a *Catch the Fire* conference at Bath City Church. It was packed with church members and visitors from far and wide, and again, they brought with them that special quality of the Father's heart.

We have no formal links with TACF, like the churches that are Partners in Harvest do, but have developed a very strong friendship. The first reason we are not currently an 'official' part of their operations is simply that we believe relationship has to be at the heart of any such arrangement and, just practically speaking, this is obviously more difficult with people in another continent. Our church had, for some years, been joined to the Covenant Ministries group of churches, and when we agreed to go our separate ways in 1996, after twenty years, a vacuum was left. So we are still, as a church, in the process of discovering our identity and our values – it is a vulnerable time: a season of transition. At the moment, it is hard to say how much of what we have learnt from Toronto is 'it' for us, or whether there are other parts of God's DNA and destiny for us that are to go alongside it. There may well be whole spheres that God wants us to be an expression of, which we have yet to discover.

Our longing is to move more deeply into both the values we began with, and the profound experience of God's presence and love which we have tasted over these past few years. Our vision is for a city-wide revival, which will touch the region around us and see many unchurched people encounter the Father who longs to have them back.

Chapter Two

What God has done in Toronto has invaded our whole foundation as a body of God's people, with a revelatory building block,
which we will never lose. It is that the only way things of lasting
value can come about is through deep dependence on the work of
the Holy Spirit. Our people have become alive again in their own
walk with God – the process John Arnott spoke of. Some have
genuinely had roots of trouble in their lives pulled out: the healing of hearts has deeply affected the church. There has been a
whole change of culture and attitude from 'principle' to 'heart',
as people have become far more aware of the Holy Spirit. The
level of His anointing on individuals' lives is much more evi-
dent, and values have changed: with mercy and kindness now
esteemed far more highly than 'being right' or 'being wrong'.
This does not in any way negate the need to hold fast to the truth
of God's Word.

Gift and talent are coming alive, as people are more moved by
God; a new freedom of creativity is emerging, as is the increasing appearance of the prophetic. Where we have felt it appropriate, we have had visiting speakers come to talk and minister on
areas such as deliverance from the demonic, curses, Free-
masonry: in the process, recovering decades of lost ground,
where our lack of understanding had kept us from receiving
God's fuller revelation. When I now consider Jesus' oft-repeated

words that He came to 'heal the broken-hearted and set the captives free', it is profoundly meaningful and real.

However, it would be less than honest not to admit that quite a few members of our fellowship have struggled with the new direction we have taken over the last few years. Perhaps they have not had an encounter with the Lord, or not experienced the refreshing power of His 'river' in the Holy Spirit. Some are disappointed that what they expected to happen has not materialised; while others feel that simply having experiences of the Spirit doesn't have a bearing on real life outside of a meeting. In all this, though, there are only a few who have felt any of this so deeply that they are no longer able to remain part of the Body.

I believe that wise pastoral care must mean incorporating these people and appreciating other points of view. We are keen to avoid any model of church which has certain criteria for being 'in' and being 'out' as its basis. However, we have made mistakes pastorally in handling the Toronto-type phenomena, in two particular areas. Firstly, I don't think we have always been discerning enough about some of the more disturbing manifestations that sometimes occur. We have, perhaps, at times, been too *laissez-faire* in our approach. Secondly, and very much related to that, some of the occurrences that people see can indeed be disturbing, at least to start with – and I don't think we have always made it clear enough to our congregation what is going on. We need to explain and interpret what is taking place, for those who are unfamiliar with such things, so that, instead of being alarmed and confused, they can feel reassured and be open to receive themselves, which is the whole point. Coming from a 'fellowship/house church' type of background, we are, perhaps, more naturally open to the idea that religiosity can keep people from a real encounter with God. However, we also need to be aware that excessive mystery also denies people the reality.

So, we have experienced some quite strong challenges from members of the church, which have had the positive effect of causing us to keep questioning the direction we have taken. Indeed, there may be valuable parts of life as a Christian that we have not pursued strongly enough, as we have been preoccupied with the Toronto direction. This can give people a poverty that they don't deserve in their Christian experience, and that is certainly something we must try to avoid.

For all of that, it is inconceivable to me that we could ever now return to simply 'doing church' in the way we used to. This whole experience over the last half decade has meant so much to me personally that, even with all the failures and conflicts, it is just too significant to ever go back. I think the members of Bath City have been fantastic in their hunger, their patience with us and their forbearance as a church. These last five years have been a roller-coaster ride, during which I have, at times, felt vulnerable, and even disappointed. But I have never once wanted to go back to things as they were.

As far as the nature of the church itself goes, what has been repeatedly reinforced for me is that the Holy Spirit builds it, not us: the initiative lies with Him. You know how it is: we can get so complicated, so organised, so religious. What I would much rather have than any of that, is simply a bunch of people who are open to be touched by God; and that is the direction in which we are moving. In some areas, we are less 'organisational' than ever.

If I had to summarise my response to the Father's blessing, I would simply want to say: 'It works!' And I think people some-times too quickly withdraw from it, when pressures of life come in. They forget the taste, and are in danger of becoming dry again. Yet, within all that God is so evidently doing, there is a tension over when to wait, and when to move, based on what God has already said. People talk about 'taking the city for Jesus', and this is clearly God's heart. Yet, the Lord repeatedly said He did only what He saw the Father doing. The effects of Toronto are spilling out everywhere, in the church and beyond, and there is a growing sense of having permission to go as the Holy Spirit moves you to. It has, for some time, been part of our mission statement as a church that we should be 'a radical community filled with God's presence', and that now means more than it ever has before.

So, as to where we see our church heading in the future, our dream is this: if we as a people are genuinely affected in our own life by God; if we are healed, and continually filled with His Spirit; then we have a lot more confidence that life in our homes and streets will be powerfully affected as well. We would like to see thriving communities all around the city, but I still see the 'harvest' primarily as taking place in homes. If we are truly manifesting the fruit of kindness, mercy and forgiveness, then this will affect the unsaved people in the city. At the moment, I feel we are still in essential preparation time. It boils down to the simple fact that if our hearts are not healed, we cannot handle God's power. I do believe, without any doubt, that God is going to send His power to this city. The more our hearts are healed, the more we can flow in His anointing.

WILLI STEWART

Willi *is an Anglican minister, who leads a new congregation called C.O.R.E. (City Outreach through Renewal and
Evangelism) in Dublin, Ireland. Willi longs to see a new
generation of Christians, passionate about Jesus, and
equipped and trained for the harvest. He is married to Ruth
and has four children.*

WILLI STEWART

Chapter One

I first heard whisperings about something happening in a small Vineyard church in Toronto, at a Vineyard leaders' conference that I attended at Ashburnham in England. Gary Best was speaking and it sounded like God was certainly up to something. However, Canada was very far away and it seemed to me to be just part of what God was doing in refreshing the Vineyard at that time.

Our plan for that summer of 1994 was to holiday in Switzerland and recharge our batteries, staying with some friends who lived there. By the summer of 1994, we had been leading an Anglican church plant, which had been going for one year. It was called CORE (City Outreach through Renewal and Evangelism). We were centred in Dublin and our heart was to reach out into the capital city and the Nation with the love and power of God. Big Vision!

It hadn't been an easy time for us. We had moved from a small rural town called Naas, just south of Dublin. We had seen a lot of people become Christians there and grow as disciples and, although I had a clear sense of being called to plant a church in the city, it was a hard move for us as a family. We came from a small growing community of faith into a city situation where, initially, anyone who belonged to our congregation lived quite a distance from us. We had no immediate neighbours and we lived, at the time, in an area of predominantly elderly people or immigrant students. On top of this, we had a new baby – number four – and my wife Ruth's mother had just died of cancer. So, we had four major life changes all at once.

However, although hard, our first year had all the hallmarks of God's mercy upon the calling, as the church grew in size and people came to the Lord. Sometime in May of that year, friends of ours visited us on their way through Dublin, telling of how our Swiss friends had been to Toronto and had experienced a wonderful outpouring of God's power at the nightly meetings which were taking place over there. My initial reaction was, 'Good – let's go to Switzerland!' Ruth, in her heart, was praying, 'Lord let us go to Toronto'. It was only a short while after this that other friends of ours heard of what was happening in Toronto through people who went to Holy Trinity, Brompton, in London. In due time, a tape arrived of Ellie Mumford's talk to the congregation at Holy Trinity, Brompton, along with a cheque from some friends, encouraging me to go over and see what was happening. Rightly, Ruth reminded me that I couldn't go alone and happily, some other financial provisions allowed us both to go over. It was our tenth wedding anniversary that year, and so the trip had particular significance for us as a couple.

We really didn't know what to expect in Toronto. There was only one ten-day section of time when we could get suitable flights at sensible prices. Who would have believed it would be so hard to get a flight to a world capital like Toronto! In the flurry of having to arrange flights, work and someone to look after the children, we didn't get a chance to listen to Ellie's tapes. We had heard, from staff, other friends at HTB, about some of the things that had happened to them, and we sensed that to spend some time in the presence of the Holy Spirit, as He worked in that church, would be of great value to us. Something in our own spirits was creating expectancy, and a longing to taste what God was doing there.

It wasn't until we had arrived in Toronto in 90 °F heat and when, suffering from jet-lag, we lay awake in the early hours of the morning, that we listened to Ellie Mumford's wonderful description of her experience of the church there. We began to feel that the morning would never come.

We arrived late for the first evening meeting we were to attend. We had a lot to learn about the lack of public transport in Toronto and the need for a car! We arrived at a very ordinary warehouse building, which, on that evening, would hold some 400 people. We had missed the worship, but we sensed the presence of God's Spirit. As we sat down, we felt that it was good to be there but, at the same time hoped this was not something crazy. The fact that this was a Vineyard church certainly helped to allay any fears. As we looked around, I think our initial reactions were, largely, ones of amusement. What struck us were the very obvious manifestations. One man leaned back on a wall looking somewhat helpless, talking happily to a woman with his right hand shaking and jumping. While in conversation, the woman's head would jerk involuntarily. As the talk began that evening, people around us would laugh, shake or appear to receive a sudden jolt as if a bolt of electricity had surged through them. Then, just in front of me, a young man slid suddenly off his chair and onto the floor, pushing his chair back into my knees. No one seemed be at all worried. I thought, 'this is mad', yet I had seen enough of the Spirit's work to know that, in all the strangeness, this could easily be God. I guess you could say that our hearts were strangely warmed. We were not quite sure what was in all this for us, yet, our appetites had been whetted, as we witnessed the joy and the power present there that night. We looked forward to our visit the next day, and we were not disappointed.

The next day was Sunday, and on that evening, a number of baptisms took place in a pool outside the front of the church. As testimony after testimony was given, we found ourselves profoundly moved, as people spoke about how the Lord had radically changed their lives. For us this was the key: we could see clearly that God was in this. Seeing the joy on their faces, as the Holy Spirit touched their lives afresh, made us feel free to receive during the meeting that night.

We were certainly willing to co-operate with God, however, there was a very real sense in which God moved sovereignly in Ruth and I. Throughout the worship, we were excited by the confidence and intimacy, which marked this time. John Arnott called some people up who had been touched, over a number of days, and he interviewed them. This, we discovered, was a nightly faith-building, God-blessing event, which seemed to allow for an even greater receptivity to the work of the Holy Spirit. As we watched and listened we saw, not only hilarious physical manifestations, but were also aware of a growing sense of awe. Just as we had listened to the stories of the people being baptised, now, again, our hearts burned within us. We were watching with several hundred other people, yet it was as if we were the two on the road to Emmaus and Jesus Himself was drawing alongside and walking with us. We had always been people who wanted to go with each wave of God's Spirit, and this occasion was no different. We had been in Toronto for twenty-four hours and we were saying, 'Yes Lord, we want to experience Your presence, we want the joy, we want the equipping'. By the time the eight days at the church were over, we had received all this, and more.

At the ministry time that night, Ruth and I found ourselves shaking, crying, jerking and rolling on the floor, as we responded to God's presence. Every time we thought we'd had enough, over would come another member of the team and pray that God would go deeper in our lives, that we would have more and the whole, physically exhausting, shaking would come on us again. I remember, on one of these occasions (they happened every time we had prayer), lying beside an Englishman, who turned his head to me and said, 'I've been lying here for an hour and a half, and I'm dying to go to the toilet – but I can't move – I can't get up'. The thought of it sent us both into gales of laughter. I tell this because, after our visit to Toronto, Ruth and I were walking through Hyde Park in London. We noticed the innocent way some children were playing together, unconcerned about the watchful eyes of parents. It struck us, as we watched, how it looked so similar to the fun and innocence of those receiving prayer. And we thought of the freedom and even abandon which God brings: no small thing, in a world that in its busy rush after other gods, finds itself bound and incomplete.

One aspect which left a lasting impression on us, was the sacrificial willingness of complete strangers to pray with us and to genuinely want us to be filled with more of God's presence and love, with no thought for themselves. We noticed how, time after time, their prayer ministry team took great delight in seeing others encouraged and refreshed. It was very much a case of them 'preferring us in love'. One man who, we found out later, came from somewhere near Niagara, prayed for hours with us during that week. The last evening he was there, we sought him out to say thank you. We thought we would see him again. Living in a small country like Ireland, you are always expecting to meet people again. His answer was so understated and such a blessing. He told us that he wasn't anyone special, he was not a leader: he had dyslexia and found himself limited by that. He reckoned we would meet in heaven, but his joy that week had been quite simply to bless whatever God was doing in our lives. I don't know his name, but each time I recount this story, I fill up with tears, as I think how this ordinary man, in ministering to us that week, was instrumental in releasing blessing to so many others when we were later ministering, back in Ireland.

The Toronto church was no self-centred church of 'bless me'. It was not a time of big names or great speakers. It had the feel of a church trying to catch up with what God was doing. The church was all the better for the innocence of it all. They understood that this was a work of God; that it was bigger than them; they just wanted to follow the cloud, pour the oil, get into the river and give away all He was pouring out. Many were the analogies to try to explain the outpouring. Back in 1994, John Wimber's longing was always to bless the Church of Jesus Christ, to see His bride made ready and this came through in what was happening in the Toronto church. I had seen this so often in John, and in the many friends we had in the Vineyard at that time. Yet, we could see that driving it all was not just a

'Vineyard' model of ministry, but an amazing outpouring of God's love. It was as if a dam of God's love and power had burst: you couldn't hold it back even if you wanted to.

Over the years, people like David Watson, Sandy Millar, David Pytches and John Wimber had all been big influences on my life and ministry. When it came to planting a new church in Dublin, we were clear that our calling was within the historic Church. However, we had been deeply influenced by the values of the Vineyard church. Consequently, when we arrived home, we found that the congregation was already open to the ministry of the Holy Spirit and expectant for more of God. It was such a delight to come home, yet one thing we wanted to do was to take others over to taste for themselves what God was doing through the Toronto church. I had also begun to understand something of the wonder of impartation. As someone who had a particular anointing would pray for another person, they too would receive from the same anointing.

We decided to charter a plane, and began the administrative headache of getting a whole group of Irishmen over to Toronto. In the end we went out on three different flights and had a wonderful week at the *Catch the Fire* conference, in October 1995. My wife Ruth went back to attend a healing conference and, two years ago, I was invited to speak at their *The Party is Here* summer conference.

Each time we returned, we were part of conferences which were at least 5,000 in size, so the whole thing had a very different feel from that first week of encountering God afresh on that first visit. Yet, on each occasion, the Lord spoke powerfully to us and renewed our love for Him, our ability to hear Him and our desire to serve His Church and the nation in which He had planted us.

What really encouraged me the last time we were there was how, in the midst of the problems with the Vineyard leadership, the media hype, and the constant flow of thousands of people, they were endeavouring to grow a church. I was thrilled to see how they were getting to grips with pastoring people, raising up leadership, steering their way through the rather unhelpfully wild individuals and groups who always accumulate around what seems to them to be a 'do what you like, renewal church'. The leaders, indeed, wanted to ensure that the renewal would continue to grow in size and deepen in quality without trying to stage-manage it. I could not think of a better couple than John and Carol Arnott to have pastored this movement. How like God to take a couple who were unknown; who had a small church at the end of a runway in Toronto, and equip them to care for this outpouring of Himself, which He wanted to use to startle and strengthen the church across the earth.

We have not felt that we should develop any formal links with Toronto. We loved what they were endeavouring to do and we know how special it is to feel linked into a relationship-based network, especially when you are wanting to be wide open to the work of the Holy Spirit. We also know how vulnerable such a church can become, in the context of denominational churches and streams, which are generally wary of any renewing work of the Holy Spirit. However, God had and has other plans for us. We continue to pray for the leadership of what is now TACF, and over the years, in our various contacts with them, we have continually found that we are united as we drink from the same river that flows from the heart of God.

Another very significant time for us in Toronto, back in 1994, was a simple intercession meeting which took place one afternoon. About thirty or forty of us came together to pray. We began in silence, asking the Lord to speak to us, and later, as we began to share, there was an incredible sense of God's presence. We found ourselves reacting physically, as we heard the Scriptures read. It was as if our bodies were saying 'amen' to God's word. A group of very proper English vicars (whom we have since grown to love and know well and have ministered with) were watching. They were bemused, and looked quite uncertain, as they watched us. Suddenly, one after another, they broke out in explosive laughter. They fell to the floor laughing and quaking, where, I believe, many of them spent a large part of the rest of the week. Some of these men, such as Bruce Collins, who is now one of the leaders in the New Wine group of churches, lead growing churches in England, and have significant ministries in encouraging and equipping the church in Europe and beyond.

During that prayer time, the lady who was overseeing it came over to Ruth. She saw that Ruth had been hearing from God. 'Prophesy, ' she said, 'speak it out, don't be afraid, put words on it'. Ruth began to shout, 'I have oil and wine, honey and wine in the Promised Land, revival and new wine'. She kept repeating this. She sensed that this was very significant for us, for Ireland and for the church: that you couldn't live on the old wine any longer or the old oil, or on old anointing. God was pouring out again the 'new wine' of His Spirit, and we needed to drink our fill. This sense Ruth had was reinforced by a word given in one of the evening meetings, where a man called out, 'Don't go back to Egypt, don't go back to Egypt'. We knew that for us there was no going back to business as usual, we could no longer simply follow some pattern: at least not for now. God ruined us in Toronto, in that He had brought us to a new place of experiencing Him and seeking after His kingdom: we were at a place of no return. For Ruth, that afternoon of intercession opened up a whole new understanding of the prophetic and intercession, which greatly helped us as we returned to Ireland.

On the last night we were in Toronto, the auditorium was packed with people: a large number of which seemed to be Anglican clergy and leaders. Ruth and I were among those who had been asked to testify to what God had done in our lives during the previous week. I recounted how, just seven days earlier, we had been sitting in the congregation amused at what we were seeing. Now, circumstances were reversed. I was asked what God had done in my life, and I felt it was twofold. Firstly, I had a greater sense of the Father's love for me, and His calling upon my life. This was something which, over the next few years, would be drawn out more and more. Secondly, I knew I had a great urgency within me to reach those who did not know Jesus.

I longed to see people come to faith and I had a burning passion to see a new generation of young Christians rise up in our Nation. As I stood to share this, I became aware of Ruth beside me becoming increasingly uncoordinated. She was being so incredibly affected by the love of God, that she could hardly stand. She looked as if she were drunk and in her drunkenness was like a little child. It was quite amazing, and totally unlike Ruth!

We had to leave quickly to catch our plane and, as she was being carried out (she couldn't stand) John Arnott asked her, 'Is this for the Anglicans'. She shouted, 'Yes, yes'. As she called out, she was making movements with her arms as if she was throwing something over them. We have often considered how blessed so many in the Anglican Church have been through the renewal, and have fondly remembered how these actions of my wife, 'drunk in the spirit', so passionately expressed the heart of God for those church leaders who had come so thirsty.

Chapter Two

Ruth and I arrived back from Toronto on a Saturday night, jet-lagged, yet excited. At the back of our minds, we wondered if what had happened to us in Toronto would have any bearing on our ministry back in Ireland. As we look back now, we need not have worried, although we could never have imagined just how significant our week in Canada would be. We had already arranged two speakers for our morning and evening services the following day, and in the morning Ruth and I really didn't have much time to say anything, except that we had had a wonderful time away, in a church where we really saw God at work.

In the evening, Steve Nicholson from the Chicago Vineyard was speaking and, having been away, we had not had time to advertise this. Up until this Sunday, the usual attendance at our evening services had been twenty to thirty people, as we were still a fairly new church plant. On this occasion, however, a couple of hundred people showed up! It was incredible. Steve interviewed Ruth and I, and we were, again, overwhelmed by God's presence. He then spoke briefly and then asked anyone under thirty to stand up. To our amazement, the aisles were packed with young people who stood for prayer. I say stood – but not for long. By the end of our evening service, the church, which was an old eighteenth-century Anglican building, with all the trappings of history, was littered with bodies. I was incapacitated somewhere at the front, and I asked Steve if he could give the blessing to formally close our time together. I guess that was a work of God in itself, a Vineyard pastor dismissing an Anglican service because the clergyman couldn't get off the floor!

From this time onwards, for the next eighteen to twenty months, our little church plant which had started eight months earlier with about twelve people, became an oasis, to which people from all over Ireland came to receive prayer and be refreshed by the Holy Spirit. During this time, I noticed the same trait I had seen in Toronto. Our congregation became a willing ministry team, to bless what God was doing in the lives of so many people from all sorts of backgrounds. They gave generously Sunday after Sunday and at conferences. Often, I meet people, even now, who comment on how deeply the Lord worked in their lives at those celebrations, and what a significant foundation was laid for an ongoing journey with God.

One of the difficulties that did emerge was that some of our congregation felt swamped. They loved the visitors, but they knew that, ultimately, those people would be involved with other churches. Their question was – who is our family community? How do we identify our home base? I knew enough about God's order to realise that, as the river of God's love begins to flow, it needs clear channels, to ensure that we, in our humanity, do not either debase God's work in the midst of the excitement, or try to control it. Either would have brought disaster. What we saw, in the midst of this wonderful refreshing, was the need to go on ensuring that we were part of enabling God's kingdom to grow, as well as developing as a church.

So, we spent time growing home-groups, equipping leaders, praying, fasting and reaching outwards into the city. This was also the reason why we did not try to have nightly meetings. The anointing was very powerful in and around us, yet we realised early on, that we were not called to copy Toronto, and also, because of our size, we knew that we would have totally exhausted our very willing congregation.

During these first couple of years, we had to deal with a lot of painful criticism. Many had their own reasons why this was all wrong, and not from God. I got letters from people who would never otherwise bother with me. Suddenly, it became important for them to set me straight. I could never understand why they had, so vehemently at times, to try to harm something that had the potential to radically impact this land. During this time, harmful videos decrying the 'Toronto Blessing', as it was known, penetrated the Evangelical Church in Ireland, confirming people's worst fears and our congregation was black-listed. I decided not to spend time answering critics. However, I believe that the large amount of negativity prevented many more people experiencing this wonderful outpouring.

For Ruth and I there were, I think, three specific areas that grew or developed, with a greater cutting edge, from our time in Toronto. These were: a wider and richer understanding of the whole area of the prophetic, in life and ministry; a much greater desire to pray, understanding the link between prayer and the prophetic; and a greater heart to be pioneers to the nation of Ireland, to see its people turned back to Jesus.

We began to discover the first of these areas, not long after we came back from Canada, when we had a team from Toronto come and visit our church. That night, the building was packed with some 600 people. Many had come just to look and, I am afraid, were unimpressed, especially some from the charismatic renewal period in Ireland, and those who came from the conservative evangelical wing. Some came believing that we were quite mad, and left feeling vindicated! Others, however, found that God 'hooked' them in a way they had never known before, and called them to follow Him.

A strange, yet profound, moment at the heart of that evening, was a prophecy given by Ruth. Over the few days before the celebration, Ruth found that the Holy Spirit seemed to be alerting her to all things green. Everything from traffic lights, to trees, to the word 'green'. What came together for her was that God was speaking about Ireland as an emerald that was making up part of His crown: it was a beautiful 'jewel in the crown'. It was about

God calling on the nation, and His desire for people to know and love Him. As she spoke, something ignited in people all over the church, some began to moan, cry, shake and generally respond with an involuntary physical 'Amen' to the word. I had not expected this, nor had I seen it before, yet it was a significant moment, which brought a new understanding and experience of the prophetic, and a desire for the prophetic to take centre stage.

The interesting sequel to this word came, I believe, six years later. We had just reopened an old church building, St Catherine's, in a fairly run-down area of Dublin. This was going to be our place of worship. One of the Irish evening papers interviewed me and did a centre spread. They came up with the headline 'Revival Bell Tolls for Jewel in the Crown'. They were, of course, talking about urban renewal and the reopening of a building. For us, however, it was a clear pointer that what God wanted to say to us had implications at all sorts of levels. Indeed, there is a sense that what we have seen happen physically, has been a pointer to what is happening in people's lives.

I should say that the arena of the prophetic within the church was always there. Ruth was always able to hear clearly something of God's heart and, indeed, our church came out of some prophetic words: the most important of which was that wonderful text of Isaiah 61:1–4 which Jesus uses to inaugurate His ministry:

> 'The Spirit of the Lord GOD is upon Me,
> Because the LORD has anointed Me
> To preach good tidings to the poor;
> He has sent Me to heal the brokenhearted,
> To proclaim liberty to the captives,
> And the opening of the prison to *those who are* bound;
> To proclaim the acceptable year of the LORD,
> And the day of vengeance of our God;
> To comfort all who mourn,
> To console those who mourn in Zion,
> To give them beauty for ashes,
> The oil of joy for mourning,

> The garment of praise for the spirit of heaviness;
> That they may be called trees of righteousness,
> The planting of the LORD, that He may be glorified.'
> And they shall rebuild the old ruins,
> They shall raise up the former desolations,
> And they shall repair the ruined cities,
> The desolations of many generations.

This underpinned a prophetic call to us. Yet, going to Toronto allowed it to blossom with a new strength, purpose and direction. As a result of it, our congregation became a hugely motivated, envisioned and committed people.

The second significant area of change for us was Prayer. This was also something we had, of course, always done. For years, prayer had been a way of life. Yet, again, as this new work of the Holy Spirit grew and deepened, so did the desire, the depth, and the drive to pray. Prophecy and a deep longing to see people saved, ignited our whole and half nights of prayer, our prayer celebrations and creative corporate intercession times. I, personally, had never dreamed I would cry as I prayed. Yet, as I did, I began to understand the apostle Paul's words to the Roman Christians that the Spirit 'helps us in our weaknesses' interceding for us with 'groanings that cannot be uttered' (Rom. 8:26). I understood how Elijah, in 1 Kings 18:42, squatted down seven times, as if he was giving birth, as he prayed for rain to fall on Israel. Yet this kind of praying happened in us, and still does when the Lord ignites a passion for the lost or the church. I guess Ruth, myself, and others, prayed before Toronto, but afterwards, we deeply desired to pray. In saying this, I do not necessarily buy into all the intercession theology which is around today, but prayer, for us, is a key to keeping in tune with God's heart.

The third major area that God ignited, was a great desire, not just to see individuals come to know Him, but also to affect the nation. It is a big vision and it is linked to a pioneering ministry that the Lord has opened up for us. For us, as a church, the call is specifically for renewal and evangelism: to see the Church in

Ireland renewed and its leaders equipped. This call was deepened, and we had a greater belief that we would again see Ireland as a country that could point others to the living God. This calling grows each year, and we are excited about it. We have also seen many people come to the Lord, especially through the *Alpha Course*.[1] However, I have to say that, as we look out on a city and nation which is increasingly lacking God at its centre, we have been disappointed that our effectiveness in seeing people come to faith in Christ has not been greater. There are many reasons for this. As the established churches in many areas have lost their authority, as the country becomes ever more affluent, as the post-modern pluralist mindset gains the upper hand, young Irish people, in particular, are looking for an unbounded life. They want to explore the previously unavailable and 'forbidden fruit' of money, sex, and power. They are not immediately asking the questions which might lead to Salvation. The renewal did not bring great numbers into the Kingdom in Ireland. Yet, it did give us a framework to believe in a God who can dramatically intervene. We also realise that the same God who gets us to wait patiently, while lying on the floor, or whatever, is the God who calls us to wait in expectant prayer and in building relationships with our neighbours. He calls us to lift our eyes to the harvest that He will bring, and for which, I believe, we will be made ready.

I have no doubt that we, as a church, are where we are today, not only because of over thirty years of Christian history for both Ruth and I, but more particularly, because of what the Lord did with us in Toronto and the consequences of it. It is hard to understand, sometimes, how the, often dramatic, encounters with God have led, ultimately, to sacrificial giving, ministry to the poor, reaching out to deprived young people, a greater desire to pray, to know God's heart, and much more. Yet, for those who willingly came forward for prayer, we have seen how God has opened up whole new areas in their lives and ministries. The finances were a particular example of this. As the wave of visitors began to ebb, we were left with a congregation of less than ninety people. Out of that group, some £800,000 was given towards our new church building, and our church budget rose to between £80,000 and £100,000. In the midst of the wonderful wildness, they gave financially for the work of the church.

Personally, I have found, more than anything, that my time in Toronto has given me a vision not only to grow a church, but to see that church effectively reach this city and nation. It is a vision that has come with a particular depth of passion. It contains within it, not only the normal understanding of church growth and the ministry of the Holy Spirit, but also something that can not be picked up from books, talks and conferences. There is an urgency, drive and passion from the Holy Spirit calling me out, inviting me to allow my life and ministry to move and be taken to that place of no return. That is why I can never say that everything has been easy – on the contrary. There is a lot that has happened over these past six years that has had the mark of the fire of the Holy Spirit. I am reminded of the words of Isaiah in Isaiah 40:7: 'The grass withers, the flower fades, because the breath of the Lord blows on it'.

We have been aware of how, when the Holy Spirit comes, there is also pain, as long-held and often well hidden issues surface and need to be dealt with. Some ten months after our first trip to Toronto, the Lord began to bring to the surface of my life long hidden pain, the presence of which had the potential to devastate my life and that of those around me. Yet, in His love and mercy, the Lord encircled me with men and women of wisdom and love. I experienced the love of the Father, and the ability of His people, born of His Spirit, to take off the tattered garments of death and to walk with me into life.

I noticed how, as the Spirit moved afresh in people's lives, He began to clear out the debris that lay around us. One girl in our congregation had a wonderful picture which was of a wave which crashed along the shoreline of Ireland and then receded again, leaving a shoreline littered with rubbish which needed to be cleared up. It seemed to describe our situation quite well. The sad thing seemed to be that the wave had receded. However, in this vision, she saw that, already, a new wave had begun to build. This picture is one that we have experienced in quite clear ways many times since, and we see in it a particular work of God's Spirit.

More than anything, I feel that Ruth and I have a much greater desire, willingness and clarity to hear what God wants for us, the Church He has given us, and the people we are called to reach. As we have allowed God to speak to us, and as He has repeatedly brought fresh words and direction into our lives, it has been with a wonderful dynamic intimacy. Often, we have been caught up into the very heart of God, and been given a confidence to say 'Yes, yes, yes', even when we haven't had a clue where this would lead. I must say that it has been wonderful to see the same thing happen many times, among the congregation.

None of this makes for an easy life. We have often found that when the Lord speaks, He asks us to get out of our comfort zone: to follow Him into a place where we can be part of bringing change to His world. This has meant following Him into difficult places. Since our time in Toronto, God has called us increasingly radically. Indeed, even as I write, the Lord is speaking about an area of compassion, which will certainly take us to a place that is out 'over the edge'!

Yet, it is these hard things, even more than the 'easy' manifestations and the outpouring of joy, tears and laughter which have given me confidence to believe that this outpouring has been clearly a move of God. It would be far easier to get back into a comfortable ministry, which could ease us along for the next twenty years. But, I think of the men and women of God down the centuries, who set their faces towards God, in spite of the personal discomfort. They are remembered today for their contribution to the Kingdom of God, although, in their own generation, they were misunderstood. We are not to be stupid, and I do not believe that something seemingly weird and unusual is, necessarily, any more from God than a thought-through, sensible, directed life. I have certainly seen, before and since Toronto, how this part of the Christian world attracts the sort of people, of whom maybe the kindest thing to say is, that I wouldn't want to go on holiday with them. Nevertheless, I would rather cope with this than the sense of death which characterises too much of the church of the West today.

As we look back now, some six years on since our first trip to Toronto, we do so from a position of deep thankfulness to God. The wild, irregular manifestations have passed, although physically, we still react to God's presence in all sorts of ways in worship and prayer. We have passed through all the controversy and, I believe that we are in a place of greater spiritual depth. The original call to renewal and evangelism within the historic church setting is still our calling, and our experience of the 'Father's Blessing' has only increased our understanding of the breadth of what this is to be. I am glad that we kept the focus on growing the church, and did not become merely a place that hosts conferences, as some folks would have encouraged us to do. I guess, in some ways, the unusual nature of what God did with us has caused the people we want to reach to keep an even greater distance from us. It is hard for many to understand us, and they are frightened in case they shake or fall. Yet, it is the Lord who got us into this, and we know that when He is at work it will, as I have said, upset everyone's comfort zones. Still, we are only starting on the journey He has for us. Paul's words, in Philippians 1:6, are important at this point: 'He who has begun a good work in you will complete it until the day of Jesus Christ'.

The great prayer of the 'Fathers Blessing' was 'More Lord'. That is still our prayer. 'More of Your presence, more of Your word, more of Your heart for this city and nation.' Yet, this means that we do not look back to some particular time or type of blessing as a final model. What the Lord did in us was and is significant. I believe the whole prayer and prophetic aspect, which flowed from God's dealings with this church, has changed us forever. We have a greater sense of His grace and of our need to rely on His Spirit for constant refreshing. Yet, 'more Lord' means that He has more for us, and the wave of His renewal is already, I believe, building around us. If we look back, it should be in thankfulness, learning the lessons He teaches us so that we can look forward to all that is yet to be. I want to be someone who is aware that 'He who promised is faithful'. Toronto was a gift of God to us, yet was not without its problems and questions. He gave us His gift at a significant time for the work He called us to do today. As we now look forward to our call into this nation, I know He will again meet us there.

NOTES

[1]*Alpha Course*, HTB Publications

STEVE HEPDEN

Steve is married to Chris and they have two children, and one granddaughter. He lives in Lancashire. For the last four years, Steve has been working as an itinerant minister to churches, and speaking at conferences in the UK and abroad. He has many years experience in leadership in the pastoral and prophetic and has a particular calling to minister wholeness and to encourage the church to come into a new and intimate relationship with God as Father.

STEVE HEPDEN

Chapter One

I first met John and Carol Arnott in 1991, on an aeroplane! We were returning together from Central Europe, after participating in a conference as part of a ministry team. There were probably about fifty of us, and it seemed as though we had taken over the plane.

A bunch of us were grouped together at the back. Something had deeply touched Carol and had affected her to the point of wanting prayer – 25,000 feet above the ground! Ministry with inner healing and deliverance is always a challenge, but when it takes place so high above the earth it also has its theological challenges! We gathered around and ministered appropriately. I don't think anyone who didn't know what was going on would have seen us, although we were not quiet. I appreciated Carol's determination to be set free, despite the difficulty of the location. Of course, it was an unusual time, but it was *God's time* and that is what counts. Who would have thought that, years later, God would take John and Carol and thrust them into a literally, world-wide ministry.

I have been visiting North America, and particularly Canada, once or twice a year since about 1983. From 1992 onwards, this also included John and Carol's first church at Stratford, Ontario, and later, the Toronto Airport Christian Fellowship. To really appreciate John's entrepreneurial spirit you only needed to look at the Stratford building and the housing development next door to it. Both were John's initiative. He had an idea about creating a dome-type church building finished with sprayed concrete on the inside. It looked like half of an enormous golf ball and was very effective. At one time there was also a Christian School situated in this unusual building. It was truly unique and made its mark in Stratford. John also initiated a scheme of very good, low-cost housing through a Christian housing association. There were a few dozen houses in this scheme on land adjoining the church, which, naturally, had a significant impact on the local community.

My perspective of Toronto comes from many years in a pastoral and prophetic, church leadership background. In the mid 1990's I was working from the base of a ministry centre, and in the last four or so years, have been itinerant. This has taken me into many churches, particularly in the UK, but internationally as well. I have also spoken, taught, and ministered at many conferences. All this has exposed me to a wide cross-section of feelings and opinions about Toronto.

John and Carol spring-boarded into Toronto from Stratford, and the next time I met them was at a conference, late in 1993. This was held in the building in Dixie Road, right at the end of the runway of the International Airport in Toronto. It was very noisy, particularly when jumbo jets took off or landed.

I was involved, with others, in a week-long conference, and John had kindly loaned us the building. It was a fantastic time, with so much happening and many leaders deeply touched. It took place not long before January 1994, and there were indications, including some prophetic words, that something big was about to happen. Some amazing miracles took place at this conference: again, possibly a foretaste of things to come, and I recall, clearly, being right in the middle of one. I had just finished one of the late morning teaching slots and we were worshipping, when a couple in their thirties came out for prayer. There was no appeal – which was unusual for the conference – they just walked out towards us. I was standing by John and

Carol, and I found myself saying to the lady that when she was in her mother's womb she had suffered a trauma. Imagine the shock, when she screamed and then fell on the floor. She was too far away to be touched by us – it was totally supernatural. As we gathered closer, we saw that under her clothes a sort of rippling was taking place. She was wearing trousers and a short-sleeved top and, from her knees to her stomach area, this sensation was clearly apparent. I remarked to John and Carol that it seemed that God was doing some deep surgery, and she screamed out again. Later we found out that there was a powerful pain released from within her ovaries. She finally got up and told us that she shouldn't have been at the meeting, but was meant to be preparing to go into hospital. Tests from her doctor had shown that she had cervical cancer and the recommendation was immediate surgery. Instead of making arrangements for surgery, she had come to the meeting. Later, she saw a specialist who confirmed that he could find no trace of cancer!

Six or seven months later, I was back in Canada again at another conference, and was telling this story. About half way through, I recognised the very woman in the congregation. What could I do but stop and get her to finish the story herself. Yes, she was healed!

The following January, Randy Clark visited Toronto, and the Spirit of God moved in that dramatic way. In May 1994, I returned to Ontario and was due to speak one Wednesday evening at Toronto Airport Christian Fellowship. I was with my wife, Chris, and some friends and I think we wondered what had hit us! The change was phenomenal. There were people from all over the world there. Of course, there were many from the USA and Canada, but it seemed that, at some of the meetings, there were more present from the UK than anywhere else. The place was heaving by the time the meeting started and the praise and worship took off. All sorts of things were happening. It all seemed very haphazard, with people basically doing what they liked. When they took a break in the worship, for the congregation to greet each other, I felt some hands on my shoulders and turned around to find a lady praying for me. I wasn't too keen on letting someone I had never met minister to me in that way, so I spoke to her and found that she was from California and was on her own. As the worship restarted, I could still feel those hands on my shoulders, but when I turned around there was nobody there! Spooky? Yes! I felt a heaviness upon me and I needed to ask my friends to pray for me before I was invited forward to speak.

It felt so occultic. Why did it happen? Why was it that so many people in the meeting just seemed to be doing what was right in their own eyes? Something incredible had happened in Dixie Road. It was as though the whole world knew something was happening, all sorts of people were turning up, and problems were occurring. But isn't it true that where the Spirit of God is moving, the enemy is always around as well? Of course, and we need great discernment to be able to deal with these things. The scripture is so refreshing that says, 'Where no oxen are, the trough is clean; but much increase comes by the strength of an ox' (Proverbs 14:4).

We became aware of the difficulties that John and Carol had to face in bringing godly order and security into that situation, without quenching the moving of the Spirit of God. We were all on a learning curve, but saw them, amidst all the strange manifestations, release a right sense of authority and yet still give the Holy Spirit His place.

Later that year I was in Ontario again and visited the Toronto church to speak. The Dixie Road building was getting far too small. I was due to speak on the coming Saturday evening and we were having a ball. I remember being between John and Carol on the front row when, suddenly, a wave of the Holy Spirit hit us and the whole row fell backwards onto the chairs. The place was like a battlefield, with bodies all over the floor. It would have been easy to remain in control and not go with the way the Holy Spirit was leading but, frankly, we would have lost out. Most who were there submitted to Him and something remarkable happened.

After things had settled down a little, a young woman asked to testify. She described herself as a lawyer: she was certainly a very 'together' woman! I recall seeing her on the floor by us. It looked as though she was unconscious. She said that while she was on the floor she had had a vision of Jesus. He came close to her and then, as it were, walked right into her. She saw, deep within her, a prison with a little girl behind bars: it was she, as a child. Jesus went through the bars into the prison, took the little girl by the hand and led her out! The woman spoke of being sexually abused as a child and knew, without a doubt that, as Jesus took the little girl out of the prison, she was being healed. Well, 'heaven came down': we had a fantastic time and I had not even preached!

In 1992, my book, *Explaining Rejection*,[1] was published. Whilst working on the book, and beyond, God had been doing a great work of inner healing and deliverance in my life. Little did I realise that further spontaneous and sovereign ministry was to come – not on the floor of the Airport Church this time, but on the chairs!

It was sometime in May 1995 that my wife, Chris, and I were having lunch with some close friends, in a very nice restaurant just north of Toronto. We were in Ontario for a couple of weeks and Ken and Lorraine had invited us out. The occasion quickly became a Holy Spirit time – a *kairos* moment – as, in the middle of the meal, Ken began to describe a major family issue, tied into a bitter root of judgement, which had clearly affected him. I nearly choked on my steak when I realised that Ken was telling me this because God had revealed to him that I had the same problem in my family. Ken is like a father to me, and I have learnt that when he has something to say to me about my well-being, I should listen. That evening, I turned the whole thing over to God and something was sown in my heart.

The next day, John Arnott had invited me to join other leaders at Dixie Road for a lunch-time meeting. There were about eighty leaders gathered at the front of the building, and I had arrived a little late. I crept in and sat on my own about half way back.

They were worshipping and the theme was 'the father-heart of God'. It was a soothing, yet powerful, time and as I opened myself up to the Holy Spirit, something happened. It was as though I went into a sort of trance, my legs buckled and, for some reason, I fell across the chairs. It was not an out of control experience but, as the presence of God was so strong, I chose to go with it.

I had taken to heart Ken's words and loving concern for me, and had already repented of my attitude of bitterness and judgement to my family. Why God waited until the next day to take the lid off, I don't know, other than the fact that I was in this fantastic atmosphere of the Father's love. At least two or three hours of deep ministry and release must have taken place on those chairs. I remember John Arnott and Ian Ross constantly coming up to me, looking after me and ministering to me. Other friends were there too, keeping an eye on me, but it was a very personal time as I made a choice to allow the Holy Spirit to have His way and heal past hurts. At one time I looked up through my tears and thought that everyone had gone home, only to realise that everyone was on the floor being ministered to by the Holy Spirit. It was one of those times! The worship was fantastic and it deeply penetrated my wounded spirit. It was as though the hurt child of the past came to the surface full of fear and loneliness. The release of pain was intense, but I felt safe with friends around me and in a place where the Father was pouring out His love in such a way.

It is one thing to visit, to look and see – but to participate, to open yourself up to be touched in a sovereign and spontaneous way by the Holy Spirit is something else! Yet, multitudes have done it too, and to me it was one of the most significant times of my life. Who cares where it happens? After that experience I don't!

Over the last three or so years, I have drawn closer to the Toronto Airport Christian Fellowship and have been asked to minister to the students of their School of Ministry. This has been a great area of development and growth for the church as, twice a year, more than fifty young people from different nations come together for a number of months of teaching and training, which includes a month of mission elsewhere in the world. Many of these young people have had a call to further ministry, and their time at the school has clearly been foundational to that. I have been asked to teach on deliverance and, more recently, self-worth, acceptance and the issue of rejection: much of it on and around the theme of the father-heart of God.

In one of the schools, about eighteen months ago, I was teaching about the power of shock and trauma: how, sometimes, it is possible to be open to demonic powers when in that state. I gave an example of how I witnessed a severe road traffic accident just two days before our eldest daughter, Joanna was married in South Africa, in 1994. Joanna was in the car with my mother-in-law. An open-back truck was being driven very erratically in front of us, when it suddenly veered across the road into the path of heavy oncoming traffic. The driver realised too late what he was doing and turned sharply to try to avoid the traffic. The truck flipped over, doing two whole somersaults! Two men had been riding in the back of the truck, and they literally flew out, as the truck, with three others in the cab, rolled down an embankment, only to land the right way up.

As we witnessed this scene, just a few feet in front of us, we began to call on the name of the Lord, spontaneously. I jumped out of the car and was first on the scene. I saw one man unconscious on the pavement and, without thinking clearly, rebuked any shock, trauma, infirmity and death, that was affecting the man. Immediately he awoke and stood up! I then ran down the embankment, where my daughter was holding a woman in her arms that had been in the cab. The woman was OK, but there was a man still in the cab who was unconscious. Again, without thinking, I carried on rebuking the shock, trauma, infirmity and death, and immediately the man awoke and climbed out of the truck. It was amazing!

Up on the roadside, we found another man who had been thrown from the back of the truck. He had a hole in the back of his head as big as my fist – he was dead. However, I could think of nothing except ministering to him. I laid my hands on his chest and, again, rebuked the same things, including death, and commanded them to leave him. Suddenly, he started to breathe very deeply within. It was as though his spirit had re-entered his body – he was alive. It was a miracle!

By now, the police and an ambulance had arrived and I, along with others, was pushed back. I found myself standing by two women who had been in a car on the other side of the road which would have been hit head on if the driver hadn't taken evasive action. It was obvious that they were in deep shock. I found myself asking if I could pray for them and, amazingly, they said yes. I commanded the shock and trauma to leave them and spoke peace into them. They changed visibly. God had touched them. The heart-breaking thing for me was that I could not get back to the man who had come back to life, and later I found out that he had died again. I know I will see that man in heaven, because I am convinced that God touched him, but there are always questions to ask!

Immediately after I gave this teaching to the School of Ministry, the students left to embark on an outreach trip. One of the teams had to drive five hours north of Toronto. On the way there their bus crashed into a small family van. The rear was totally smashed in, and the father, who was in the back of the van, was in a bad way. One of the students climbed through the broken rear window and saw that he was in great shock and had gargling noises coming out of his throat. The Holy Spirit was powerfully present and she laid hands on him and said, 'In the name of Jesus I take authority over this and rebuke the spirit of shock and trauma'. The man began coughing very loudly and then fell completely silent for a time. For a moment she thought he was dead, then she prayed, 'Father, I pray in Jesus' name that You will breathe Your breath of life into him.' Immediately the man took the biggest breath she had ever seen and opened his eyes and looked at her. He couldn't stop staring at her. He thanked her, but couldn't understand what had happened. We do!

Later they found out that he and his family were absolutely fine.

It is amazing that the incident was so similar to my testimony. The students had received something and had no idea that, only a few hours later, they would be called upon to put it into practice! The heart of the School of Ministry is to disciple and to enable the baton to be passed on to the next generation. That had happened in a dramatic way and, in my opinion, is one of the keys to its success. We need to mentor the next generation and I know that John and Carol have taken many risks to let this happen. It is a privilege to assist them in this.

What is astounding about TACF is that there is still an incredible momentum to seek God and to see Him move powerfully in unbelievers as well as believers. It continues to amaze me that, after six or so years, people from all over the world are still coming to receive. Granted, in the mid-week meetings the numbers are not so great as they were, although the larger conferences are still full. Yet, when I was there a few months ago, there were visitors from many nations and that was mid-week! History will tell what lasting impact has been made around the world, but what ever is said, it is a fact, that millions of people have been affected by this move of God.

To see the inexperience of those early days, in the small building in Dixie Road, change to the sensitive pastoral handling of thousands of people in their new building, testifies to the stature and maturity of John and Carol and their staff. It would have been easy to see this area of renewal just become a ministry, without much reference to the local church. Thankfully that has not happened and, although there were pressures in the early days, steps have been taken to gather the church together in a cell structure so that, amidst its worldwide impact, local integrity is not lost.

To summarise – I believe we are witnessing a move of God that is helping to inspire the worldwide Church to greater things. As we are touched by the Father's love, in this context, it can only enable us to move into the reality (at last!) of the 'Great Commission' and provoke us to 'love one another'. In this move of God, so many leaders, as well as members of their congregations, have had a new release of faith to see the miraculous, healing and deliverance, and a desire to see the supernatural power of God expressed. Most of all, has been a desire to live with a greater passion for Jesus than they have ever had before.

Due to John Arnott, particularly, I have been inspired to reach out to the lost and see them come into the Kingdom of God. He loves leading people to the Lord and takes every opportunity to do so! In John and Carol, I have seen a release of compassion and mercy for the hurting and broken-hearted. They have affected many people around the world because they have an ability to transcend culture.

We have seen: a group of ordinary people handle over three million visitors in the past six years; accelerated church growth (at least in British eyes); an administrative ability blossom; and great spiritual leadership, hand in hand with fantastic worship leading – particularly in the larger conferences. The unusual has taken place – some say bizarre – yet amidst all the pressures, fears and doubts which some have had, the leadership of TACF, in my opinion, have shepherded the local people and visitors with integrity and skill.

Have there been mistakes? Of course, and, as far as I am aware, there has been an honest response and an effort to put things right and be open for help, if and when necessary.

Most of all, I have seen and personally experienced, a 'Niagara' of the Father's love coming from a church where the leadership is not afraid to go beyond the limits in allowing the Holy Spirit to move as He wishes. Sometimes that has been against the religious status quo – for which I am thrilled!

NOTES

[1]*Explaining Rejection*, Steve Hepden (Sovereign World)

Chapter Two

There is no doubt that many parts of the world have been greatly impacted by all that Toronto has received and then released to others. There are now other strategic churches that are carrying this perspective of renewal in their own inimitable way, and it is as though they are acting as hubs, drawing together other churches and many people. These churches have really caught the heart of Toronto Airport Christian Fellowship, which is the heart of God. To me, the heart of Toronto is not just God walking in the midst, but God dwelling in the midst!

This can be interpreted not just as a visitation, which in itself is fantastic, but more as a habitation of God which we all long for. There is much talk these days about the need for the restoration of the Tabernacle of David (Acts 15:15–17), in the sense that we need to see a tremendous release of worship without hindrance. What David longed for was the habitation of God in Zion and that is why his desire to bring the Ark of the Covenant to Jerusalem was so great (2 Sam: 6). He finally fulfilled his desire, but not without cost. It is one thing to have God break through in blessing, but quite another to have God stay! I am convinced that what has happened at Toronto is but a prelude to much more, and we can thank God for the overflow. But no one I've met is satisfied to remain where they are. If we can see Toronto as a means to an end, a provocation to seek God for more and not just as a quick fix, we just might get somewhere. I, like you, want God to do much more – but are we ready? Could we handle what might come our way? All that has happened at TACF is for our learning as well. Let us take heed and push on!

Who would have thought, though, that God would chose a fairly small group of Canadian men and women in Toronto to draw His people closer to His heart? Surely, it should have been the British or maybe the Americans? But no, God will do what He wants to do!

Who would have thought that thousands and thousands of British people, including many leaders, would take the long trek across the Atlantic to visit a church at the end of an airport runway?

Some have been asking, 'Why go to Toronto?' 'Why have all these Britons spent so much money to be cooped up for four or five days in a building in a foreign land, attend meeting after meeting, and then go home?' The answer is: it has to be God, and the testimonies of people who somehow 'found themselves' there and were totally blessed – some to the point where they had to be carried out of the meeting – would fill many more books.

There is no doubt that 'Toronto Fever' affected many, and the only option was to go and see what was happening for yourself. That became the way in for the hungry and thirsty. Maybe it was the only place that one could go to and get release? I know of many leaders who will never be the same again because of the amazing emotional release and the healing that took place. Perhaps the British needed to leave Britain in order to deal with that hindering 'stiff upper lip'? But, whatever the reason, they came back healed, or on the way to healing, changed, and hungry for God. Such transformations provoked others to buy an aeroplane ticket and go. I would be interested to find out how many were first time flyers to Toronto. Whatever reason people had for being there, the fruit was undeniable and that is the most important factor.

There has been an outcry too. Can it be God? Is it of God? We have all had to face it. I have heard more about manifestations than anything else. It's such a pity that so much of our focus has been on these, rather than simply on the Father's love. There have been dogs barking, lions roaring, chickens clucking, and I don't know what else! In the early days, someone quipped that Toronto was more like a barnyard than a vineyard! There were, and regretfully still are, accusations of a wrong spirit, or control, or ungodly behaviour. But, as someone once said to me, 'Where God is moving, the enemy is not that far behind.' He seems to know that where God is blessing he can come in to distract in many ways and try to divide the Body of Christ.

We have a propensity to write off that which we don't understand. If we've never seen something done that way before, then it must be wrong. I have no doubt that some things went on that were strange and bizarre – maybe they were not of God. But why highlight these minor issues when something major that God has initiated is happening? I remember being spooked and wondering whether it could really be of God. I had to face this. Is Toronto a demonic deception? Is there a wrong spirit behind it? Do we support it? Do we speak against Toronto?

I came to the conclusion that, if you cut out the apparently strange and somewhat bizarre incidences in the Bible, you would be left with something bland and devoid of life. Consider the trance, yes trance, which Peter fell into in Acts 10 and 11. He saw a blanket come down from heaven with multitudes of animals on it. Not once, but three times! Peculiar – but it was God's method of delivering an important message to Peter that changed his heart and resulted in the release of the gospel to the Gentiles. Look also at the Pentecost experience in Acts 2. This must take the prize for the most bizarre encounter of the supernatural! If I hadn't read about it in the Scripture, I would not have believed it could possibly happen: 120 men and women in an upper room – some say that it was in the Temple. Suddenly they are confronted by a tornado that manifests inside the room, not outside the building! Then fire appears and tongues of the fire go to each person and it appears as though their heads are on fire. No one was left out. If that was not enough, they were sovereignly and spontaneously filled with the Holy Spirit and spoke in languages that they had never learned. No wonder they ran out into the street! Yet, that was what God wanted to happen, because the consequence of that incredible baptism of the Holy Spirit was the release of the gospel to the nations. What a strategy, and what fruit! Three thousand converts in one day and a further two thousand a few days later. Who cares about manifestations if 5,000 people come to faith in Christ through repentance in just under a week!

I think we have had things out of proportion. Some of us have fixed our eyes on the wrong issue. I am not saying we should ignore every odd manifestation, or blindly accept everything that we don't understand without question. But I would encourage those who still question, to consider first those things that they know to be right: the many new births, the healings (both physical and inner), the growth of the church, the impartation of an anointing that has gone around the world affecting multitudes of other churches. This is the substance to start with!

Amidst my fears, apprehensions and almost unbelief, I broke through and have now visited Toronto enough times to know that what is happening is of God. Relationships help too. Having worked with John, Carol, and others, including Marc Dupont and Ian and Janice Ross, I see men and women of integrity, as vulnerable as you or I, and certainly open to receive help where appropriate. I see a desire for the best in God, a longing to get it right and I know that they are, just like the rest of us, prone to make mistakes and admit them too! One of John Arnott's gifts is to make room for the moving of the Holy Spirit. This is risky living and may lead to consequences that have not been foreseen. But he is not alone and, besides having Carol alongside him, there is an excellent team working around him. To me this is the strength of Toronto. There are quality people around and, if things get a little out of hand, there is someone there to bring godly order, rather than let it go by, through fear, which many of us have known.

Ask yourself this question. Would you prefer sterile,

antiseptic, bland, lifeless meetings, or ones with so much life that they could develop into Acts 2:4 type experiences? I know which I would choose! Being with Jesus was incredibly dangerous. You did not know, from day to day, what you would encounter. Would it be raising the dead today? Or more demons cast out, or rebuking a Pharisee? Jesus kept surprising everybody, even His disciples. He would do things differently, like eating at the wrong house, talking to the wrong people, talking to trees or the weather, and healing on the wrong day. Wherever Jesus was there was unpredictability, and didn't it just make people feel uncomfortable! Life was not boring!

The attributes of God are amazing! He is constant in character, but unpredictable in action. We are often constant in action and unpredictable in character! Maybe we need to change? And change is all about getting out of our comfort zones. Perhaps Toronto has given us an opportunity to do just that!

Consider the four men who took a roof off to get to Jesus. I expect there was a law to cover that! They ripped someone else's roof off to get their friend healed. Desperate men take the roof off to find Jesus. Are we desperate enough to break through? What a fantastic problem it caused, or was it a fantastic solution? As well as the roof, it tore the lid off their culture, cut to the heart of a religiousness that was controlling their society, and created a miracle.

Someone once described God touching their life as being, 'seized by the power of a great affection'! This is the initiative of God and I feel that this has happened to me. I know that, for me, Toronto has served to amplify this. The atmosphere there just invites God to move on lives powerfully and for His glory. Surely, He wants to touch us in such a way that we are never the same again. Are there people, who believe in Jesus but are no longer 'astonished', 'devastated', 'ruined' or 'amazed'? Is the spirit of mediocrity on us? So many have returned from Canada totally overwhelmed by the love of God and seemingly manifesting all sorts of things. The manifestations have been less pronounced recently, but the overwhelming love is still there! Is

Christianity dangerous, unpredictable, uncontrollable, wild, threatening and outside the norm to us? Or is it as bland as usual?

I asked myself, whilst writing this, if I had ever been critical of Toronto. I don't know, but I was certainly apprehensive at the beginning and maybe somewhat fearful. Was I ever shocked? Of course! But wherever I've worked in full time ministry, there have always been times when I was deeply shocked and concerned about what was going on. You get through those times by trust and the grace of God. I now know that God is bigger than I am and undoubtedly has more surprises up His sleeve for the Church!

The issue of manifestations can be a diversion and has been a snare for some. Some have sought the manifestations rather than the Lord and have brought the work of God into disrepute. We need to concentrate on that which is more central and foundational to Toronto: the father-heart of God and passion for Jesus. I have seen and heard so many people who have testified to having a deeper and more intimate relationship with God as their father. There is, within us all, an inner yearning and longing for more of God. The Bible describes it as 'deep calling to deep' (Ps. 42:7) and Toronto has been a place that has resounded with, and satisfied that desire.

It wasn't so many years ago that certain books of the Bible, such as Song of Solomon, were hardly ever looked at, and were even virtually banned in some places, because of the perceived erotica. Yet, the renewal has helped bring about a fresh revelation and love of Scripture. So, the Song of Solomon has now been examined in its right and correct perspective. However important the physical and erotic interpretation is, there is something else, which is fantastic! The Song is a love story between God and Israel and, of course, the Bride and Bridegroom – the Church and Jesus. Similarly, TACF has been the place where a greater degree of the incredible love God has for His children has been revealed and allowed to flourish.

If you consider the impact of the beginning of the Song of

Solomon you will understand just how radical this love is and how it is that it has broken into so many lives through Toronto.

> 'The song of songs, which is Solomon's. Let him kiss me
>   with the kisses of his mouth –
> For your love is better than wine.'
>
> (Song of Solomon 1:1-2)

This is the song of all songs, the supreme song, the most excellent of all songs, a song of love and of uncommon passion. A song of songs to draw us into the holy of holies to commune with the King of Kings and Lord of Lords! The song begins with incredible intimacy: the kiss of the mouth. This is a most personal response of bride to groom, and if we go beyond the physical, we see here a desire for unity and union. It is infatuation, spiritual union, first love, the cry of the apostle, 'that I might know Him'. This is the bride reaching out to the groom for more, for depth, for intimacy and is the cry of our hearts to our heavenly Bridegroom that the union might be so strong that it becomes permanent. This has been the foundation in the move of God at Toronto. So much of what they do revolves around the Father's love and this incredible passion for Jesus.

One commentary clearly states that the 'kiss' is the word from the mouth of God to us. It is as though God kisses us with His 'rhema'! The scripture is clear: 'It is written, "Man shall not live by bread alone, but by every word [rhema] that proceeds from the mouth of God"' (Matthew 4:4).

Coming from a background of rejection and inner pain, this is music to my ears: that, at last, we can respond to God as Father, and with a passionate love to Jesus, without the pressure of condemnation, insecurity and the fear of rejection and failure. To see, as I have seen at TACF, so many worshipping and responding to God as Father, without inhibition, and often, being healed without realising it, is fantastic. I have seen men and women letting go of ungodly control and freely finding the love of the Father that has somehow eluded them for years.

It is possible for us to get to the place where, day by day, we live by the kisses of His mouth. This is the love of God – so extravagant and lavish – and it is this love which ignites a passion in our hearts for more of Him. It becomes irresistible, contaminating – even outrageous! This must be the paradox of irresponsible passion!

The father in the story of the prodigal son, behaved in a culturally irresponsible fashion. He acted more like a mother, as he ran to his son and kissed him, but it was that very act that touched the broken son and loved him into healing. It was outrageous, yes! This sort of passion is not manufactured. It comes from a grateful heart touched by grace. It bubbles up into a torrent of thanksgiving in response to a Father who will run to us and kiss us. This is the heart of Toronto.

There has been an amazing response to Toronto worldwide. People have been caught by the vision for renewal and have been incredibly touched, often very deeply. I meet and hear of people that have had a dynamic, emotional release, which has brought a freedom in their spirits and, hence, a walk with God that they have never had before.

Whatever has been said, it is a fact that multitudes have come into a deeper understanding and revelation of the father-heart of God, a passion for Jesus and a love for the scriptures that is continually bringing fresh revelation. This has been a foundation, from which Toronto has played a major part in inspiring people to evangelise with a reality that has been missing for years; to develop worship as an integral part of church rather than just a 'bit' of singing at the beginning of the service; and to move in and see a release of the supernatural with its accompanying gifts of the Holy Spirit. The reality is borne out in many testimonies, worldwide, of God moving dramatically and powerfully.

I see too, the impact Toronto has made in bringing unity to the Church rather than disunity. Being in the large conferences, you are not concerned about denominations, networks or traditions. They become irrelevant, as an amalgam of Christians worship and respond to God together. Racial, social and religious issues are just not there!

Another important aspect to this move towards unity is the response of the Gentile church to Jewish believers. I believe that this controversial issue is being highlighted more than ever in our days, and the leadership in Toronto are seeking to handle this with integrity, carefully considering how we Gentiles can open ourselves up with humility to Messianic Jews. There is one plan and purpose of God to bring unity to Jew and Gentile believers and, accordingly, TACF is open to the wisdom and direction of the Holy Spirit to play a part in bringing this to pass. Holding conferences is one way that this will happen, and is already occurring.

There has been reaction and opposition to Toronto and, in some measure, this continues. To some, this has been very disappointing as Christians criticise other Christians. It seems to fly in the face of Scripture. Where is the loving one another so that 'all will know that you are My disciples' (John 13:34–35)? Others would comment that if there were no opposition to renewal or revival they would question its authenticity.

There is no doubt that many churches that were affected in the early years of the 'Toronto Blessing' have lost something of the impact of those days, and that things are fading. In all of this, there was some conflict and division, and this in itself may have contributed to a pulling back. Accusations regarding a wrong spirit, control and deception still arise occasionally, but mainly this is from a small minority. I still come across a lack of understanding, which tends to breed fear, apprehension, suspicion and mistrust. I would now recommend to these churches and individuals that they visit Toronto. I have noticed that the vast majority of people with uncertainties who do visit are reassured.

BIBLIOGRAPHY

Alpha Resources, *Alpha Course* (HTB Publications)

John Arnott, *The Father's Blessing* (1995, Creation House)

Geoff Bullock, 'I Will Never Be The Same Again' (1996, Word Music)

Gerald Coates, *An Intelligent Fire* (1991, Kingsway)

Steve Hepden, *Explaining Rejection* (Sovereign World)

Mark Stibbe, *Times of Refreshing* (1995, Marshall Pickering/ HarperCollins Religious)

Tommy Tenney, *The God Chasers* (1998, Destiny Image)

Ravi Zacharias, *A Shattered Visage* (1990, Wolgermuth & Hyatt)